The Art of Dimensional Embroidery

by Maria A. Freitas

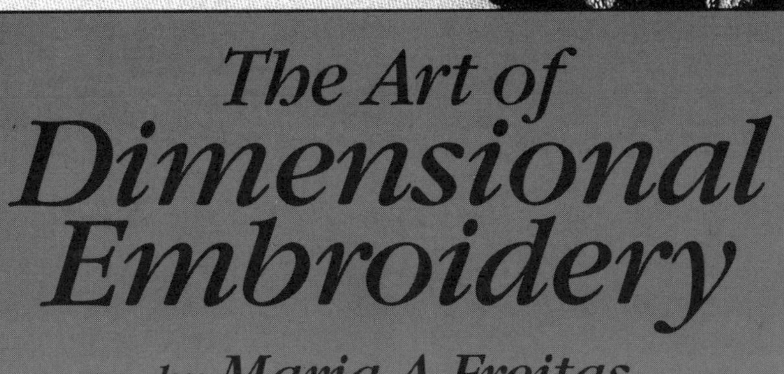

The Art of Dimensional Embroidery
Second Edition

Illustrations by	Edson and Maria A. Freitas
Edited by	Carol DeFreitas
Revised by	Adriano DeFreitas
Cover conceived and stitched by	Maria A. Freitas
Cover designed by	Karen Cook
Cover photography by	Wayne Smith Photography
Printed by	Bob Baker Reprographics

Published by EdMar Company
P.O. Box 55 Camarillo, CA 93011-0055

ISBN # 0-9639481-0-5

Printed in the United States of America

10 9 8 7 6 5 4 3 2

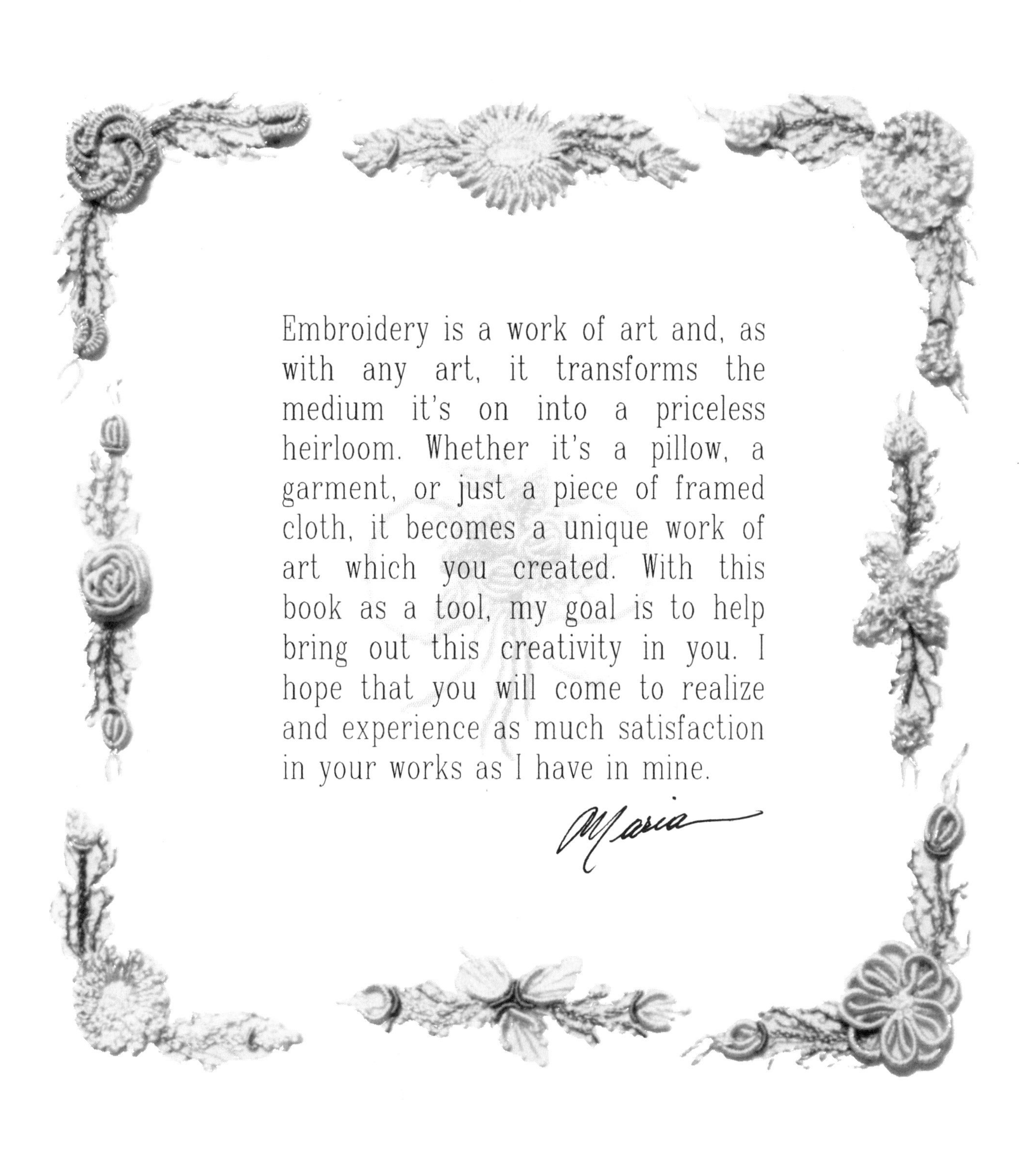

Embroidery is a work of art and, as with any art, it transforms the medium it's on into a priceless heirloom. Whether it's a pillow, a garment, or just a piece of framed cloth, it becomes a unique work of art which you created. With this book as a tool, my goal is to help bring out this creativity in you. I hope that you will come to realize and experience as much satisfaction in your works as I have in mine.

Maria

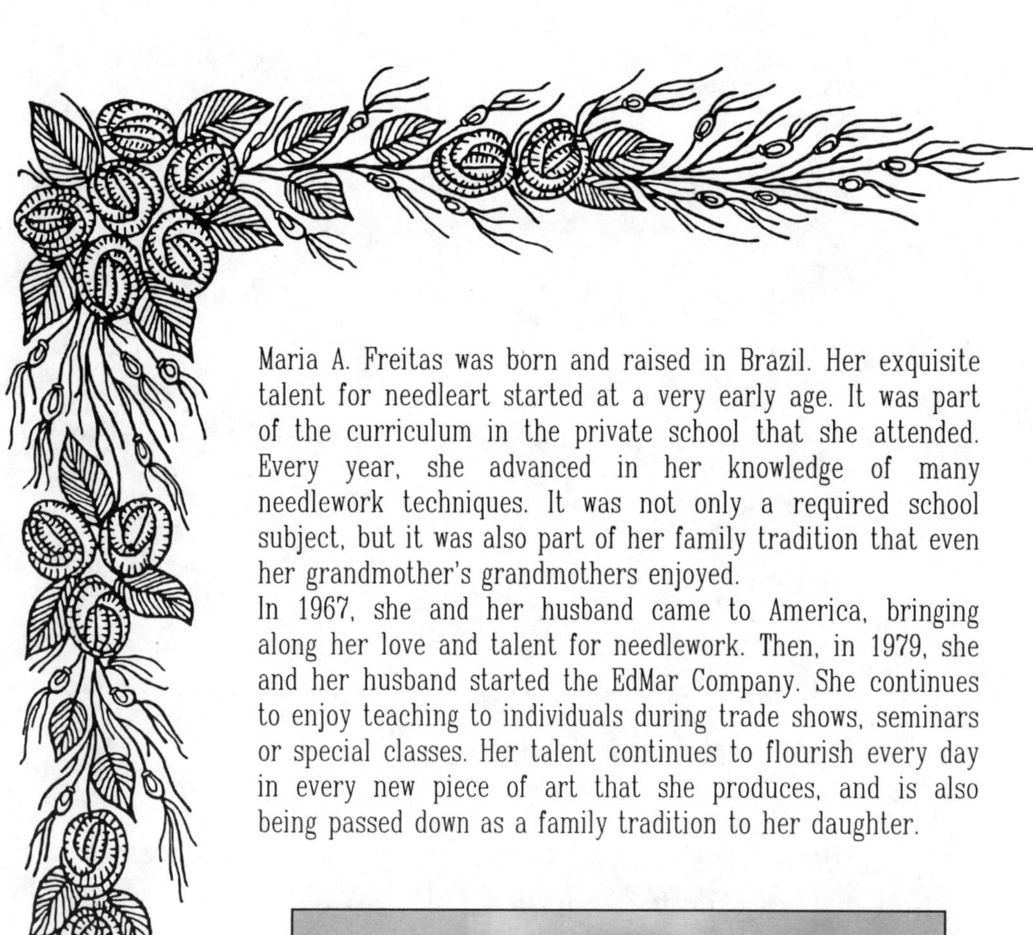

Maria A. Freitas was born and raised in Brazil. Her exquisite talent for needleart started at a very early age. It was part of the curriculum in the private school that she attended. Every year, she advanced in her knowledge of many needlework techniques. It was not only a required school subject, but it was also part of her family tradition that even her grandmother's grandmothers enjoyed.

In 1967, she and her husband came to America, bringing along her love and talent for needlework. Then, in 1979, she and her husband started the EdMar Company. She continues to enjoy teaching to individuals during trade shows, seminars or special classes. Her talent continues to flourish every day in every new piece of art that she produces, and is also being passed down as a family tradition to her daughter.

This book is dedicated to Edson, my husband. To my children, Adriano and Carol for their love, assistance, and support throughout all the years of workshops, seminars, taking and giving lessons, stitching, designing, and being wrapped so much in the threads.

A special thanks to my daughter, Carol, for her help and talent in stitching, choosing colors, and writing.

In addition, I would like to thank all of the wonderful people I have had the privilege of meeting and whose art and needlework have also graced my life.

Preface

Embroidery, in its most basic terms, has been with us since time immemorial. Over the centuries, basic stitches have evolved into the more complex and elaborate needleworks we know today. Embroidery of any kind uses stitches known and used for hundreds of years in countless ways and for many different purposes. Brazilian Dimensional Embroidery is no exception. The difference is that it doesn't limit itself to specific stitches: it uses stitches from all types of needlework. Brazilian Dimensional Embroidery is a style of embroidering where you can choose from the whole palette of stitches and knots you know.

Another difference in this style of embroidery is the thread. Rayon was introduced in the mid 1800's and by the turn the century, was the first man-made fiber in full production. Although it is man-made, rayon is not a synthetic fiber but regenerated natural fiber (cellulosic material, generally wood pulp). Rayon has long been the preferred thread for this style of embroidery because of its sheen and smoothness. Most stitches, especially bullions (which are used extensively for their dimensional effect), are much easier to make because of the thread's smooth texture.

Now we come to the question if the stitches aren't Brazilian and rayon isn't Brazilian, what does Brazil have to do with Brazilian embroidery? Well, many times throughout history, credit goes not to the inventor, but to the ones who popularize an item. Brazil started producing multicolored rayon threads in several weights. The popularity of the thread spread rapidly throughout Brazil to the point where variegated rayon embroidery became know as vari-cor embroidery. It wasn't long before the rest of the world noticed its popularity and immediately adopted it as "Brazilian".

The EdMar Company started manufacturing variegated rayon thread here in the U.S. and has witnessed its steady growth in popularity, not only for Brazilian Dimensional style embroidery, but in all areas of needlework. Today there are many organizations and an International Guild that are exclusively dedicated to the art and advancement of Brazilian Dimensional Embroidery.

CONTENTS

Welcome to the Art of Brazilian Embroidery

Thank you for purchasing this quality EdMar product. Be sure to ask your dealer about our full line of embroidery support products including books, kits, videos, plastic thread organizers, spring hoops, and a wide range of needles which include darners and platinum milliners needles.

EdMar threads are available in the following weights in over 180 colors

Thread	Weight	Ply
Glory	Fine	2ply
Iris	Medium	2ply
Frost	Medium	3ply
Lola	Heavy	3ply
Ciré	Heavy	3ply
Nova	Very heavy	6ply
Bouclé	Knotted	4ply

The difference between Lola and Ciré (See·**Ray**´) is that Lola has a tighter twist. They will each give a different look to stitches you make. Bouclé (Boo·**Clay**´) is generally reserved for special textural effects but may be applied to any kind of stitch.

EdMar rayon threads are colorfast and have a higher twist and sheen than other threads used for hand embroidery. The threads work up quickly, easily and with amazing versatility allowing you to use it for smocking, cross stitch, needlepoint and all other needle arts.

General Instructions

Opening & Storing Skeins

To open the skein, move the tag to one side to reveal the knot.You can cut through the knot or on both sides of it. The strands will then be about one yard long. The threads can be steamed with a steam iron to smooth out the wrinkles and small kinks. Lay the strands flat out on a thick cloth and gently run the hot steam iron over them.

Threads can be put in an EdMar plastic organizer or hung from the tag. To store it in the plastic organizer, cut the knot and slide off the tag. To insert the thread into the slot, use a skein threader; a long plastic strip bent on one end or a hooked wire. Insert the hook through one of the long slots, fold the skein in half over the hook and pull it up the slot. Pull it slightly over the seam under the label leaving the folded part of the thread showing. Trim the sides of the tag leaving the name and color number for reference. Insert the tag into the top small slot over the thread. Each plastic organizer will store 16 skeins. To keep the thread hanging from the tag, cut off the knot and pull on one side of the strands to make one side longer than the other. Insert a crochet hook or a piece of plastic strip bent on one end through the label where the thread was pulled longer. Bring the long strands to the hook and pull them through the label (tag). Even up the ends and pull the loop against the tag. When one strand is needed, just pull it from the loop under the tag.

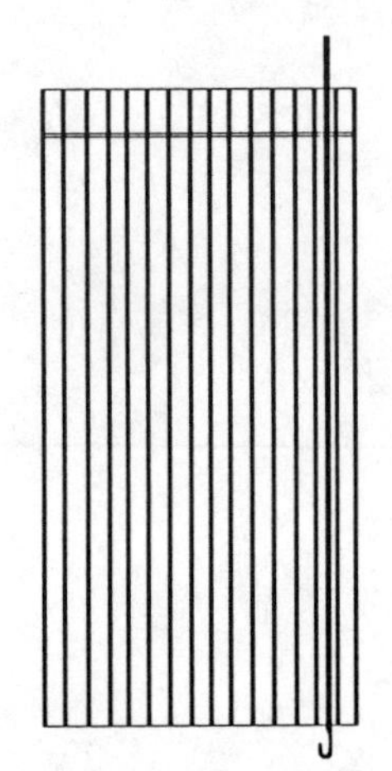

Plastic organizer

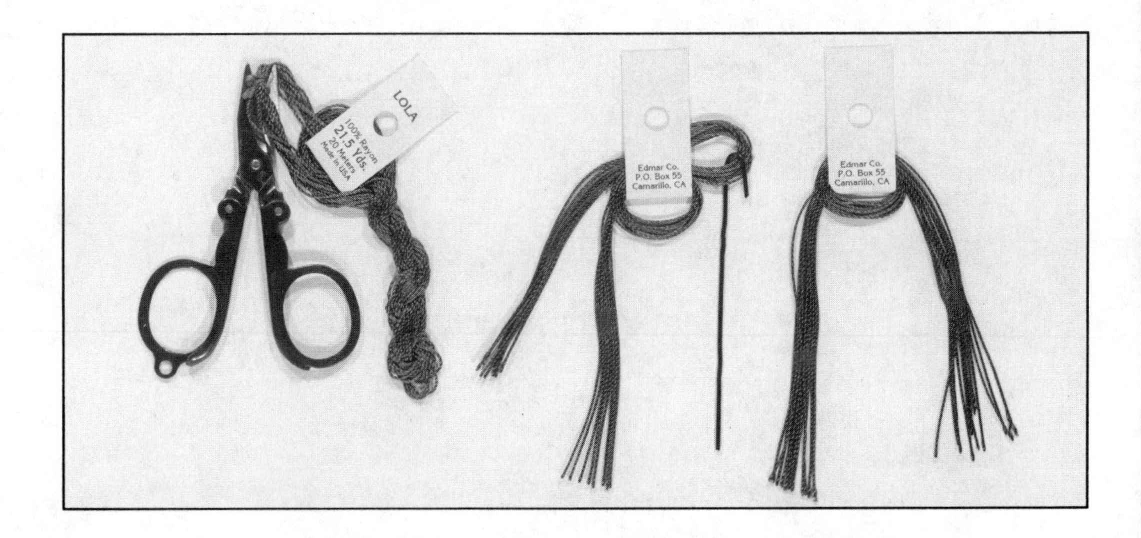

Patterns & Needles

Tracing designs from books to be stitched can be done for your own use, not for resale purposes. Remember that most designs are copyrighted. A regular pencil can be used or water erasable pens. Use a very light hand when tracing designs to the fabric. Tracing designs to dark fabrics can be done with a white sewing pencil or can be traced to wash away plastic which melts away leaving no traces when you wash your project.

Milliners needles are mainly used because the eye area is not enlarged. The eye area graduates into a point evenly allowing the thread and needle to be pulled through bullions easily. Darners are used for thick threads and to give a lace effect to stitches like cast-ons.

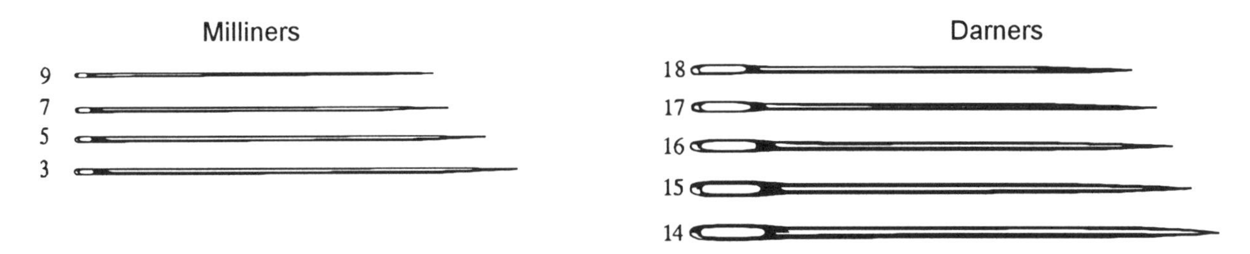

Additional guidelines

« EdMar Rayon threads are to be used as they are, never split the plies.

« Separate the threads by thickness and colors in daylight and check the number of strands with the color list. Two needles are included, a large needle for heavy thread and a smaller one for medium or fine threads.

« We recommend that the embroidery be worked with the fabric held taut in a hoop. Work stitches with uniform tension to prevent the fabric from puckering.

« The threads can be steamed with a steam iron to smooth the wrinkles and small kinks. Lay the strands on a towel and gently run the iron over them.

« Rayon threads are very slippery and one end of the thread will unravel more than the other. To find out which one unravels, get the two ends together and twist them back and forth between your fingers 3 or 4 times. The one that unravels the most is the side that should be knotted or weaved before you start stitching. At the end of your stitches, secure your thread by knotting or weaving. When tying a knot, make it small and very secure.

« Stitches should be worked clockwise and from left to right. This will keep the thread from unravelling and fraying.

« Before making any stitches that require wrapping the thread like bullions, roll the threaded needle counterclockwise in between your fingers in order to unwind the twist of the thread a little. Wrapping the thread clockwise for the stitch will then twist it back to normal. Without doing this, the thread will be wound too tight, kink up and possibly break.

« Bullions and cast-ons should be wrapped loosely on the needle. You don't want them so tight that you can't pull the needle and thread through. The thickness of your bullion is not determined by the thickness of your needle; it is the weight of thread you are using and how your bullion is "pulled". You don't want the individual wraps separated so all bullions should be pulled nice and taught.

« When making bullions or cast-on stitches, secure the threads on the back before starting the next one. This will prevent a "chain reaction" if one of the other stitches break.

« Try to keep the back of your project clean and organized. Avoid "jumping around", threads will show onto the front like a shadow if you do. Eliminate loose ends by securing them down.

Stitching Sequence

Leaves
Extra care should be taken to make sure you stitch your leaves with very even and neat stitches. Sloppy leaves can ruin an otherwise immaculate work.

Stems
Stems are worked in Stem Stitch. Stems lead from the ground up to the flowers, buds and leaves. The stem line can be stitched into a leaf to create a vein.

Flowers and buds
These should be made to the size required to completely fill their space on the design. If the design has flowers with stems, make them connected.

Branches
Branches can be made with the same thread as the stems or finer. Branches do not have flowers, buds or leaves. They only have field flowers and fine growth on them.

Calyx
This is the green part underneath a flower or bud connecting it to a stem. It is usually made with the same thread as the branches.

Fine Growth
Lines for fine growth are not printed onto the fabric to keep the pattern clear. Feel free to add fine growth to your work wherever you like. They sprout from the main branches.

Field Flowers
These are made with French Knots in groups of two or three or in a wisteria pattern (larger bunches of five or more). They add a final touch to your work.

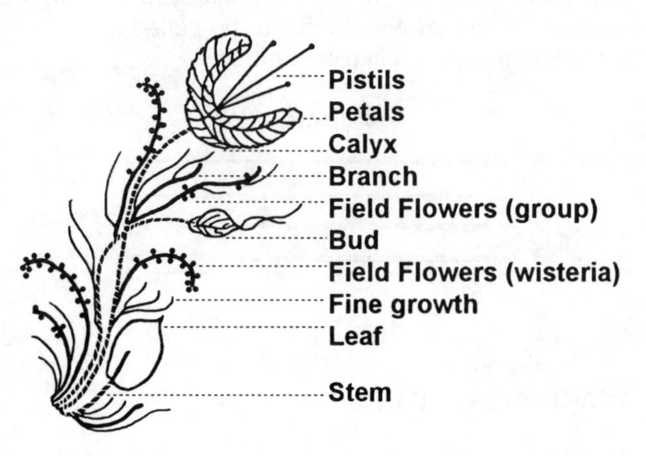

Washing instructions

The high quality of the rayon threads manufactured by EdMar makes it possible to hand wash or dry clean your finished embroidery project. Wash completed embroidery projects only. Never wash the skeins by themselves or half finished projects. To hand wash, soak the embroidered article in warm water and mild detergent for 15 to 30 minutes. Use a detergent recommended for colors and avoid bleaches. Rinse once and then soak in water and detergent again for at least two hours. Rinse several times in cold water until all of the detergent is gone. To restore the sheen of the thread, mix three tablespoons of white vinegar per quart of water in the last rinse. Roll the embroidered article in a towel and squeeze it without wringing. Standing on the rolled towel is very effective in removing the excess water from the material. Spread it out flat in the open or on a stretching frame to air dry. **Never** leave damp embroidery in the towel, folded or bunched together. If necessary, you may iron it face down.
In the event that the fabric is stained or colors have bled, boil the item in water and detergent for at least five minutes and follow the rinsing steps. Since no thread is 100% colorfast in every circumstance, follow washing instructions closely. The faster the article dries, the less chance there is that staining will occur.

To press, lay embroidery face down on a thick dry towel and press lightly so that stitches are not flattened.

Stretching the fabric tight is very important if you are going to frame your needle art. Use a hard board the same size as your frame to stretch the material. Foam board is recommended for this and can be found in most hobby & craft stores. First, lay the backing material over the board and then the fabric. Fold all the excess material around the back of the board. Secure everything in place with thumbtacks and turn it over. Using a needle threaded with non-waxed dental floss, come up on one corner of the fabric and catch the opposite side pulling the floss to stretch it very tight. Continue stitching back and forth, much like lacing a shoe, until you reach the other corner. At the end, knot it and cut. Do the same with the other two remaining flaps of material. If you're having difficulty, most craft stores can frame your work for you or help you.

Lifting the petals on your finished work can be done by spraying a small amount of fabric sizing over the flowers and then lifting the petals. Or spray it on your fingers and touch the petals lifting it. Sizing can be found in the laundry department at most supermarkets. If your needle art will be exposed without glass protection, it can be sprayed with a dust repellant. Use it on pillows, frames etc. Do not use it on mats or paper because it may stain.

Stem Stitch

Come up at A and pull through. Go down at B, up at C and pull through. Go down at D, up at B in the same hole and pull through. Work the next stitch by going up on the line and backstitching to the last stitch. Make the stitches small, especially where the line curves. ALWAYS hold the thread ABOVE the line being worked or the thread will unwind.

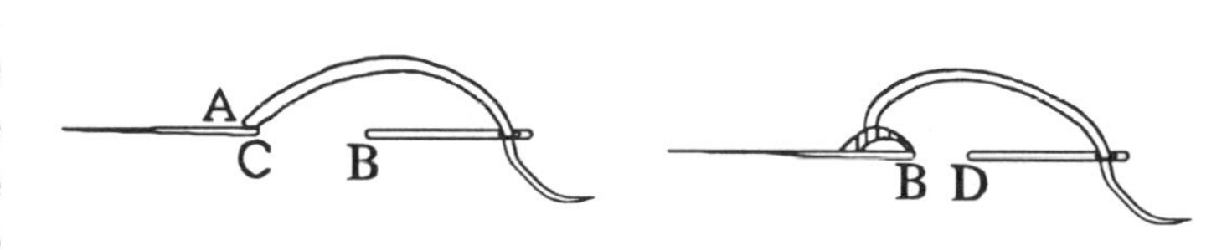

Stacked Stitch

Bring the needle up at A. Keeping the thread above the needle, insert at C and back up at B. Pull through. Next, insert the needle at E, come up at D and pull through.
Go in at G, up at F and pull through again. At the end of the line you are working on, insert the needle at point H and come up between that point and G. Pull through.
Turn your work upside-down. Keeping your thread under your needle, follow the same pattern of stitches again from A to H. Do as many rows as needed to fill your area. Remember to turn your work right side up or upside-down for each row. Every time the work is upside-down, the thread will be kept under the needle during your stitches. For large areas, the thread will unravel slightly so you may need to twist it back.

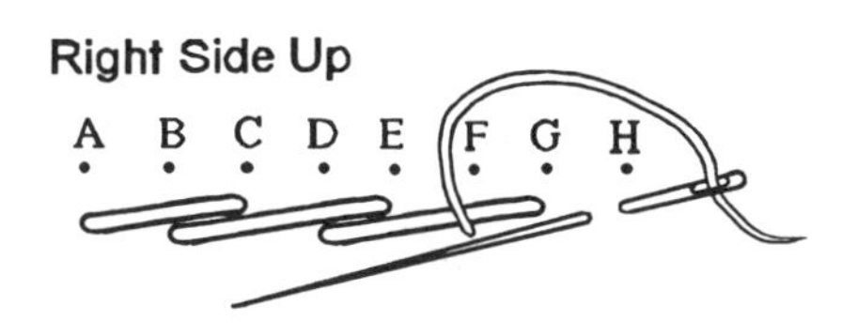

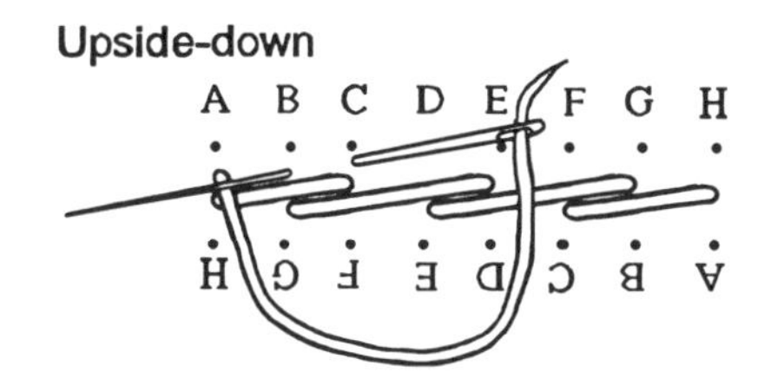

Couching Stitch

Come up at one end of the branch and down at the other end. Come up 1/4 to 1/2 way down the branch and pull through (1). Allow enough slack in the thread to follow the curve. Go down in the same hole on the opposite side of the main thread (2). Do as many catch stitches as needed to secure the branch (3).

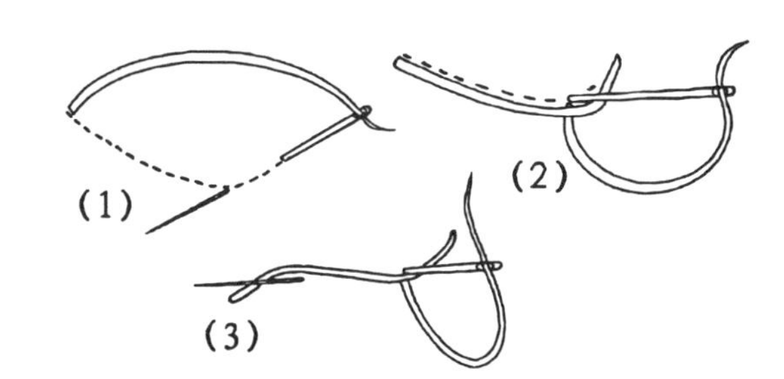

French Knots

Pull the needle up through the fabric. Holding the thread with your left hand, wind the thread clockwise around the needle 1 or 2 times. Keeping the thread taut, go back down where you came up, pull through and secure.

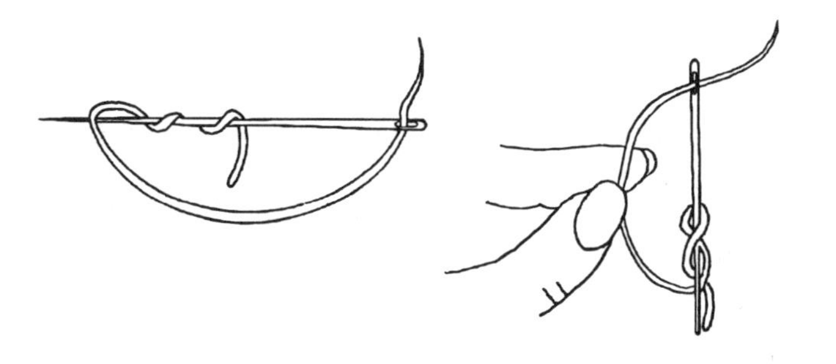

Pistil Stitch
Long Leg French Knot

Come up at A and pull through. Hold at the desired length, B, and wrap the thread clockwise around the needle 3 to 5 times. Insert the needle at B. Holding onto the slack, pull the needle down through the material keeping the thread taut.

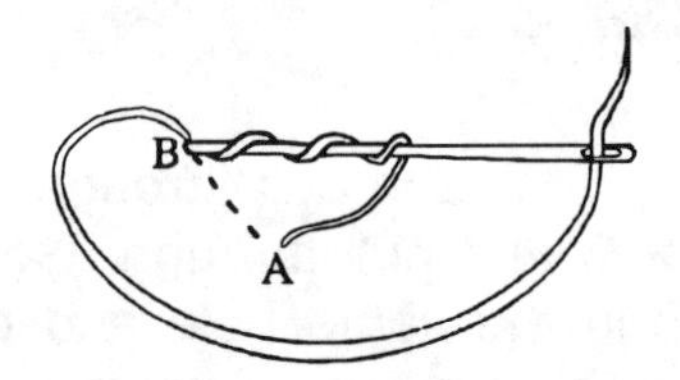

Buttonhole Stitch
Blanket

Come up at A and pull through. Make the thread loop to the right. Insert the needle at B and bring it out over the thread at C. Pull the needle through with the loop under the needle. Insert the needle at D, out at E, and pull through.
Repeat the steps until the area is filled.

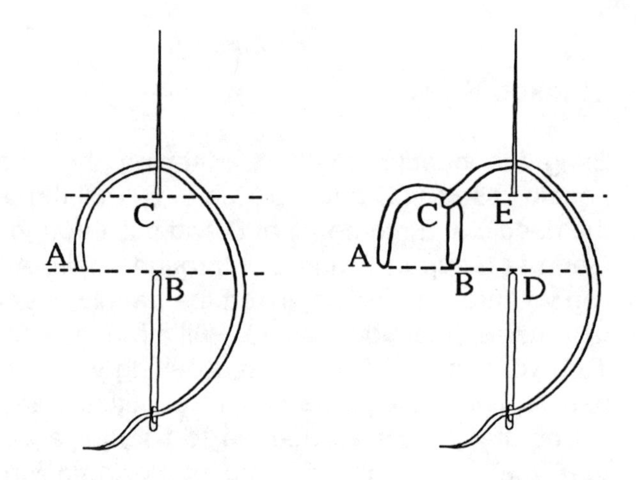

Wrapped Buttonhole Stitch

Come up at A and pull through. Go down at B and up at A. Wrap the thread clockwise around the needle 5 or 6 times. Hold onto the wraps and pull the thread through. Go down very close to the last stitch and up next to the last small Bullion.

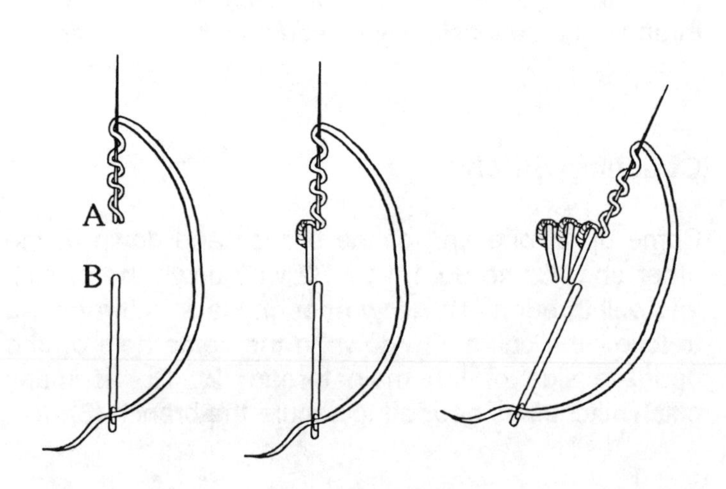

Herringbone Stitch

Come up at A, insert the needle at B and come up at C pulling through (1).
Insert the needle at D and come up at E pulling through (2).
Insert the needle at F, then up in the same hole at B. Pull through (3).
Repeat the steps until the area is covered.

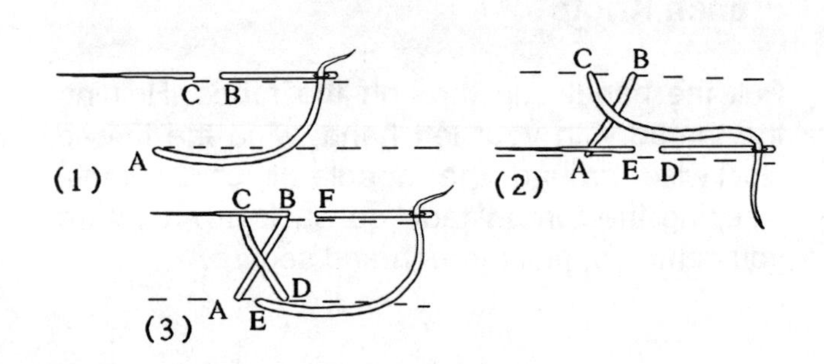

Detached Buttonhole Stitch

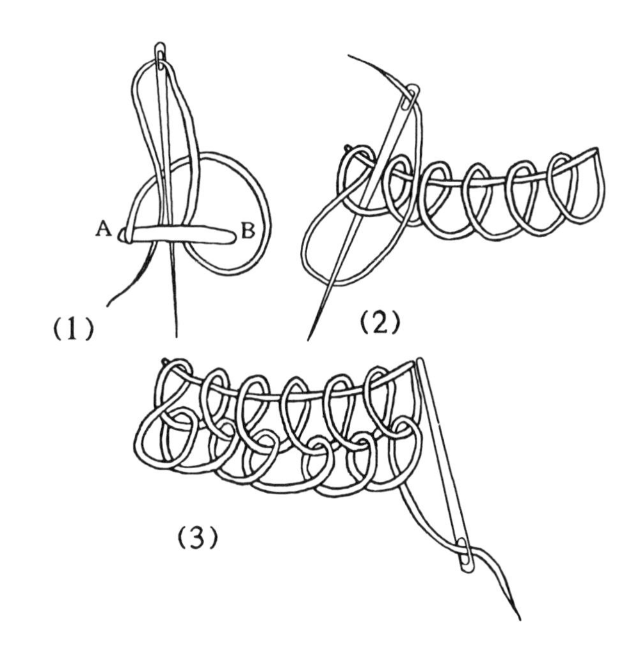

First row- Make a bar coming up at A, down at B and back up at A. Pull through. Slide the needle under the bar and over the thread to form a loop. Do not catch the fabric or thread and do not pull the loops tight against the bar. Keep the loops fairly loose. Repeat the steps for the remaining loops (1).
Second row- Turn your work upside-down and repeat the first row procedure. Make one loop on each loop of the first row (2). Do not pull the loops tight. To finish, go down at A in the same place the stitches started (3).

Bullion Stitch

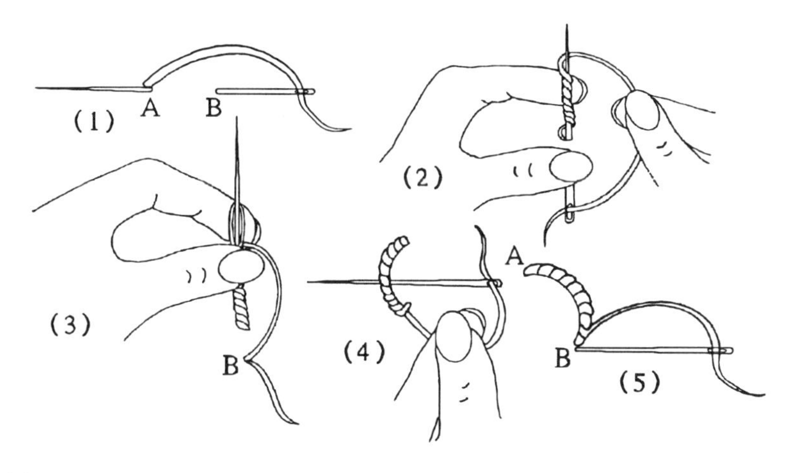

Come up at A and pull the thread through. Insert the needle at B and up at A. Do not pull through (1).
Lift the needle away from the material and wrap the thread clockwise and loosely around the needle. Do not overlap the wraps (2).
Gently hold onto the wraps and pull the needle and thread through (3).
Let go of the Bullion and pull the bullion towards B. Keep pulling the thread until it is tight and smooth.
If the Bullion gets lumpy before securing, slide the needle under and lift it from the fabric. Work the needle back and forth and keep pulling on the thread (4). Go down at B and secure (5).

Hint- Before you start any stitches that require wrapping the thread around the needle, unwind the thread a little by rolling the threaded needle in the opposite direction in which the thread is twisted. This will relax the twist and will prevent the thread from kinking and forming tight loops at the end of the wraps. All Bullions made with EdMar's rayon threads MUST be wrapped clockwise or it will unravel and fray.

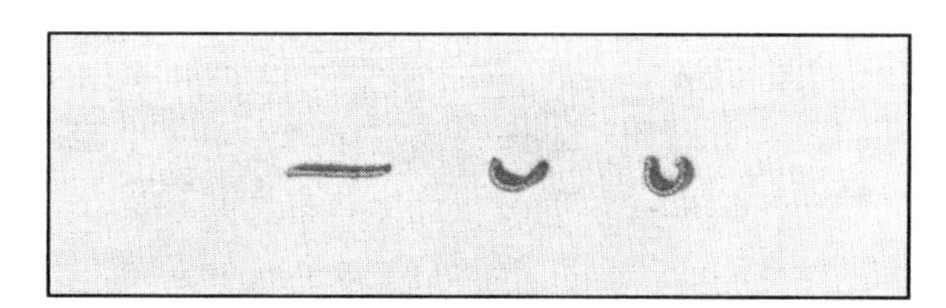

The Bullions pictured here were made with 20 wraps each. The initial bite of material for each was as follows, left to right; 1/2", 1/4", and 1/8". All were made with Lola thread.

Detached Bullion Stitch

Make a row of stem stitches (1).
Come up at A and pull the thread through. Insert the needle under the first stitch. Don't catch the fabric. Hold in this position and wrap the thread on the needle to form a bullion (2). Pull the needle through the wraps and insert it under the second stitch to make the next bullion (3).
For the second row, come up at point B on the left side of the previous row, then follow the same procedure as the first row (4).

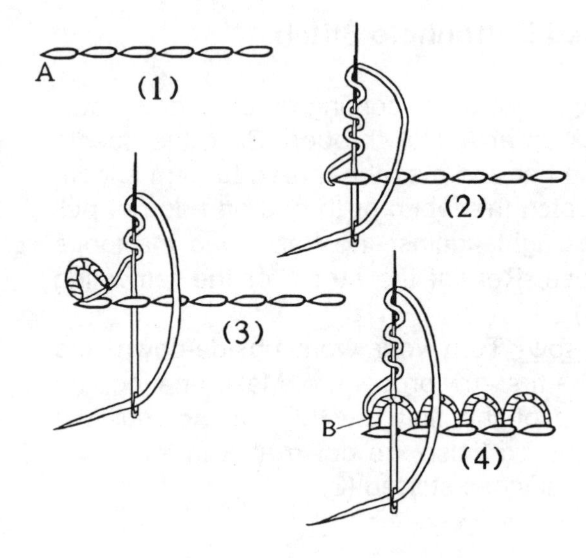

Long Leg Bullion Stitch

Running Bullion Stitch

Come up at A and pull through. Insert the needle at B, up at A and wrap the thread around the needle clockwise 5 or 6 times forming a bullion. Hold on to the bullion and pull the needle through, bringing it down to B. Insert the needle at C, come up at B at the end of the previous bullion and wrap the thread again forming another bullion*.

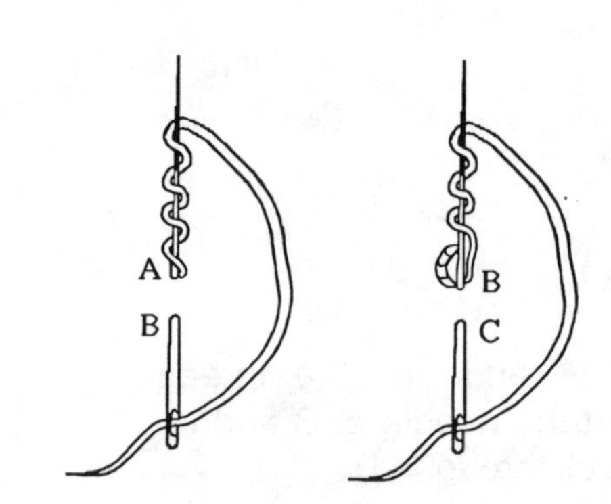

Chained Bullion Stitch

Hoop suggested.
Come up at A and pull through. Insert back down at A and up at B. Keep the needle in this position and wrap the thread clockwise around the needle as many times as needed. Hold the wraps close to the fabric and pull the needle through forming a bullion.
Go down at the base of the bullion at C and come up at the tip of the bullion at D. Hold again in this position and wrap the thread clockwise around the needle as many times as needed. Make as many repetitions as needed. To secure the final bullion, go down at the tip of the bullion*.

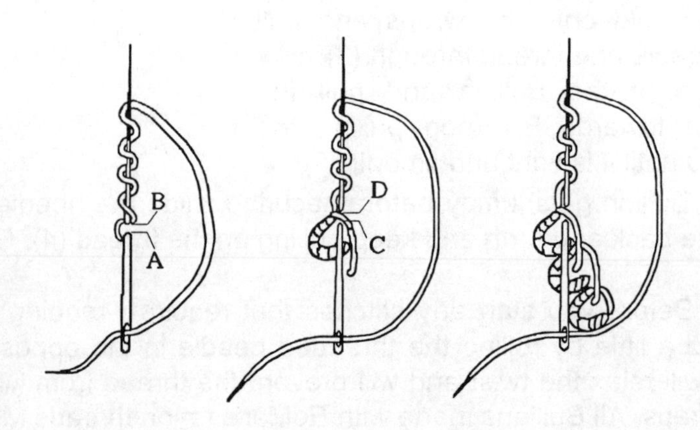

* Two different effects can be made with the bullions; you can have a straight row of bullions by adding as many wraps to fill the bite of fabric, or you can add more wraps to obtain a scalloped effect.

Cast-on Stitch

Come up at A. Insert the needle at B, then back up at A. Do not pull through. Hold the needle with your right hand. With your left, loop the thread around your index finger and place the loop around the needle. Remove your index finger from the loop and pull the loop to the needle.

Make all of the cast-ons required. Hold the cast-ons with your left hand and pull the needle through. To secure it, go back down at B. Use a darning needle for lacy looking stitches. Do not cast-on too tight or it will be difficult to pull the needle through.

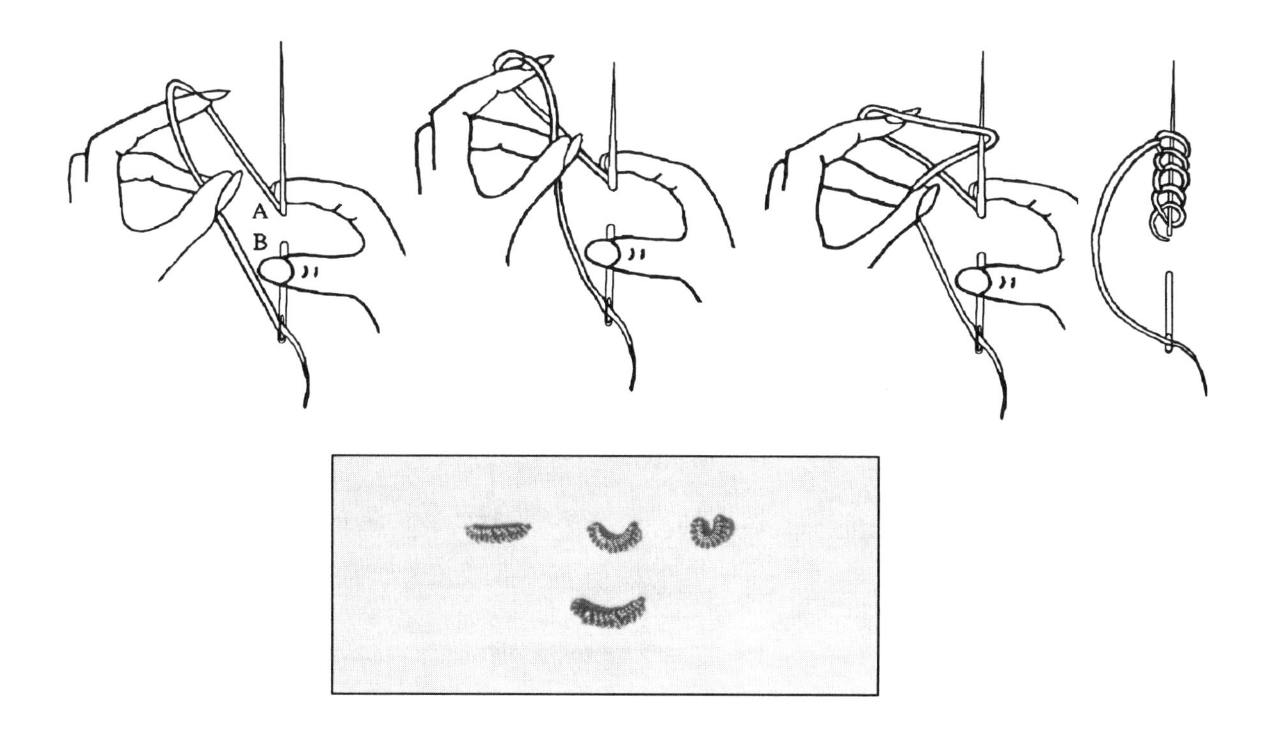

The cast-ons that are pictured were made with 15 casts for each length. Top row left to right: 1/2", 1/4" and 1/8" bites with a #3 Millinery needle. Bottom cast-on: 1/2" bite with a #18 Darner needle for a lacy effect. All were made with Lola thread.

Double Cast-on Stitch

Thread one strand of thread in a needle and knot the two ends together. Come up at A. Insert the needle at B, then back up at A. Do not pull through. Follow the procedure for cast-on stitch, alternating each side; first the right side, then the left. Do the number of cast-ons needed. Even up both strands. Hold on to the stitches and pull the needle through. Go down at B to secure.

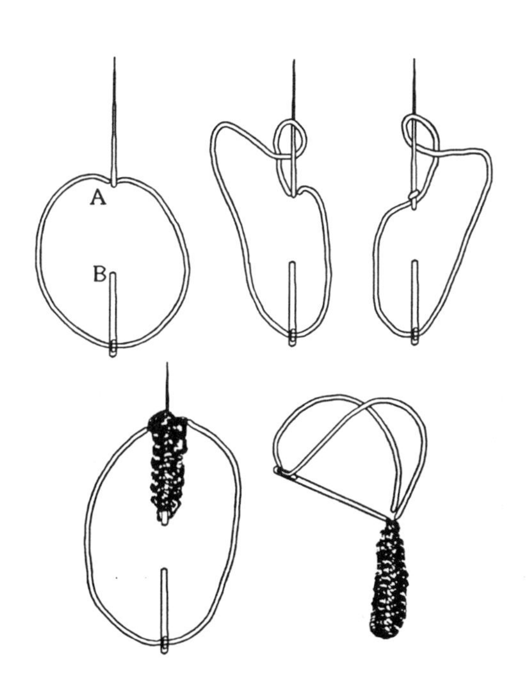

Knotted Cast-on Stitch

Come up at A, then insert the needle at B and back up at A. Hold the needle with your right hand. With your left hand, loop the thread and wrap twice around the needle. On the third wrap, insert the needle through the loop and pull through. Do the number of knotted cast-ons required and secure at B.

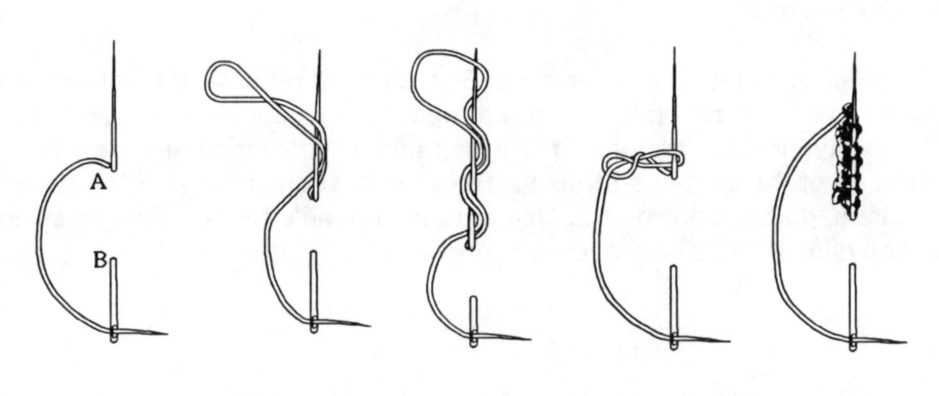

Knotted Double Cast-on Stitch

Thread one strand of thread through a needle and knot the two ends together. Come up at A and pull all of the thread through. Insert the needle at B, then back up at A. Do not pull through and lay the two strands on either side of the needle.
Hold the needle with your right hand. With your left, hold the thread as you would for a regular cast-on stitch. Wrap the loop of thread around the needle twice, then cast-on as you normally would pulling the knot against the needle and downward.
Holding the needle with your left hand, repeat the procedure for the right side. Continue alternating sides until you've done the number of cast-ons needed. Even up both strands. Hold on to the stitches and pull the needle through. Go down at B to secure.

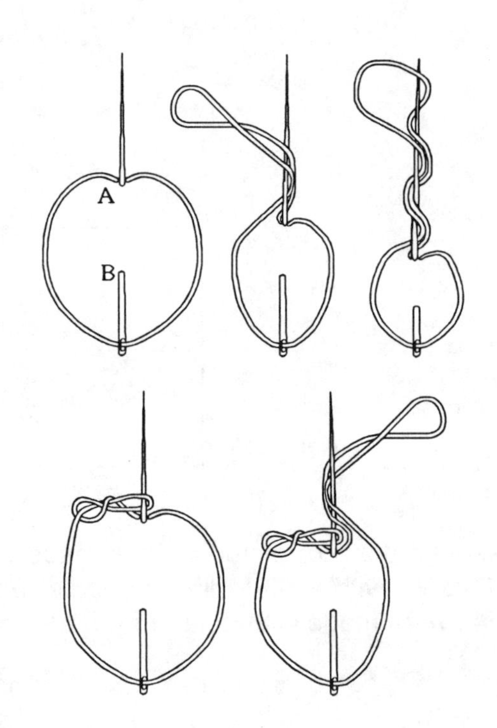

Turkey Stitch

Without knotting the thread, go down at A from the top of the fabric then up at B. Pull the needle through but leave the tail of the thread sticking up about ¼" to ½" (1). Go down at C, then up between A and B (2). Pull through just enough to leave a small loop. Make three loops the same way. Make the fourth stitch catch a small piece of material and make a locking stitch by pulling the stitch tight (3). Repeat the steps until the area is covered. Cut the loops and trim evenly, then rub it back and forth until it gets fuzzy (4).

(1) B A

B A C
(2)

(3)

(4)

Satin Stitch*

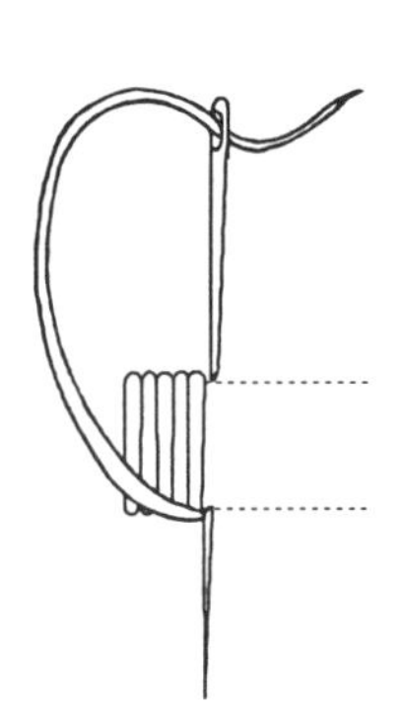

Hoop suggested.
To make the stitches even and without puckering, the fabric must be kept very taut in a hoop. This stitch is a filling stitch that covers an area with straight stitches placed one next to another. Stitches must be made smooth and with even tension. Stitch from left to right. The outline must be made very clear with a definite edge.
Come up at one edge of the area and carry the thread across to the other edge. Return underneath the fabric coming up next to where the previous stitch emerged to make the next stitch.

*For instructions on making a padded satin stitch, refer to "Acorns" on page 43.

Alternating Satin Stitch

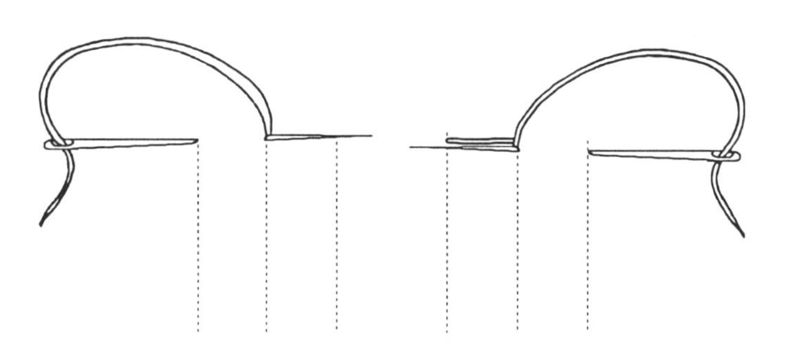

Hoop suggested.
Come up at the top of the center line and pull through. Go down at the edge, pull through and up at the center line. Repeat steps for the opposite side. Fill out the area desired making one stitch to the left side and one to the right side. Make the stitches very close together. This stitch can be applied to any shape that has a line dividing it.

Straight Stitch

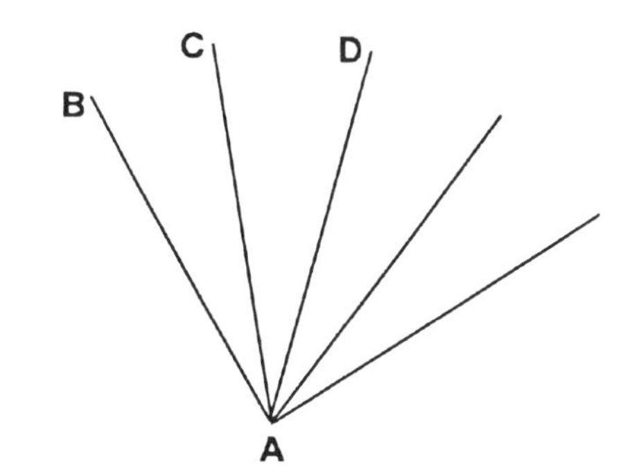

Hoop suggested.
These stitches can be worked in any direction, length, and shapes. Come up at point A and carry the thread across to point B. Go back underneath the fabric to point A. Continue going from point A to point C then back to A and so on. If a thread is carried underneath from B to C, a "shadow" will show through the material.

Padded Stitch

Hoop suggested.
Using a heavy weight of thread or a doubled medium thread, fill the area with chain stitch. For heavy padding, add more layers of stitches over the first one. Only the first layer should be stitched to the fabric. The other layers should be stitched catching only the thread of the previous layer.

Chain Stitch

Hoop suggested.
Come up at A and pull through. Loop the thread to the right. Insert the needle in the same hole, come up at B and pull through. Loop the thread up to the right and go down the same hole the thread is coming out of and up at the next point; pull through. Repeat the steps as many times as needed. To hold the last stitch in place, go down outside of the loop and pull through to the back.

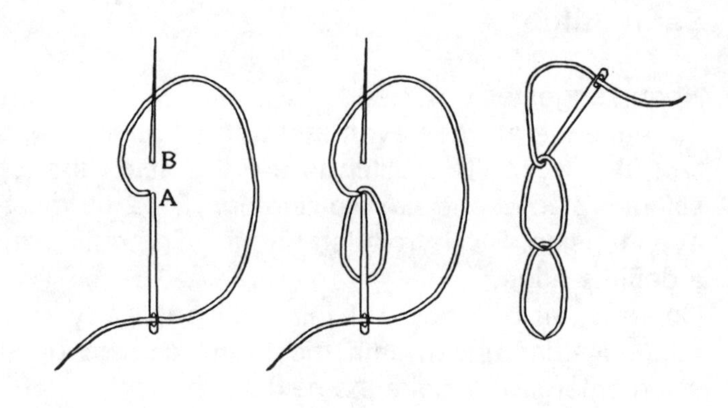

Lazy Daisy Stitch

Hoop suggested.
Come up at A and pull through. Loop the thread to the right. Insert the needle at A and up at B above the looped thread; pull through. Go down at B outside of the loop to tack the stitch down.

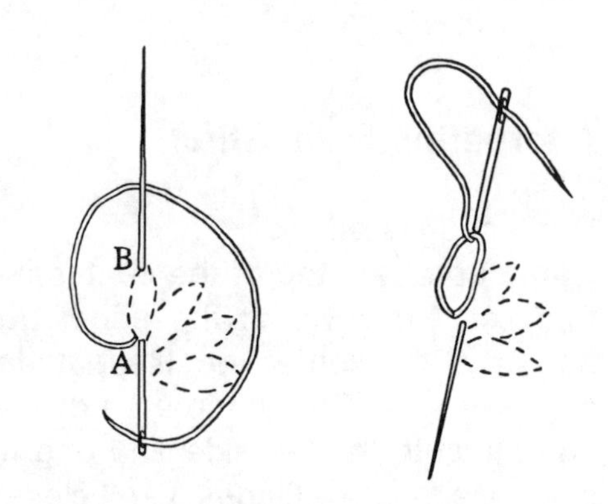

Knotted Lazy Daisy Stitch

Hoop suggested.
Come up at A and pull through. Loop the thread to the right at the tip of the petal. Insert the needle at A and bring it up at B. At this position, wrap the thread clockwise around the needle four or five times. Hold on to the wraps and pull the thread through. Go down at the tip of the wraps and come up at the bottom of the next petal and repeat the steps until the flower is complete.

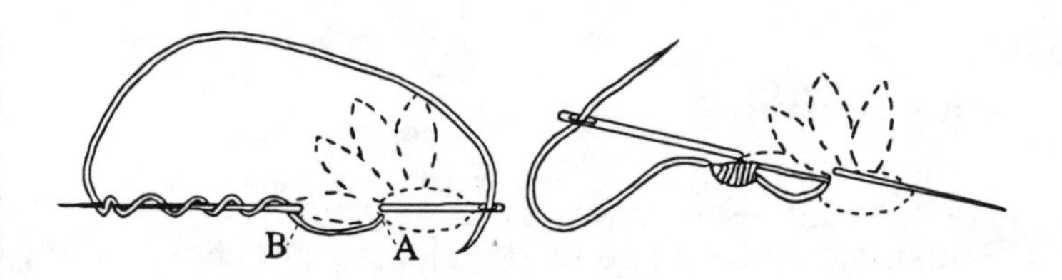

Feather Stitch

Hoop suggested.
Come up at A and loop the thread down to the right. Go down at the end of the first line at your right and pull through. Loop the thread down to the left and go down at the end of the left line. Continue going right and left to the last line.
At the end, go down, pull through and secure.

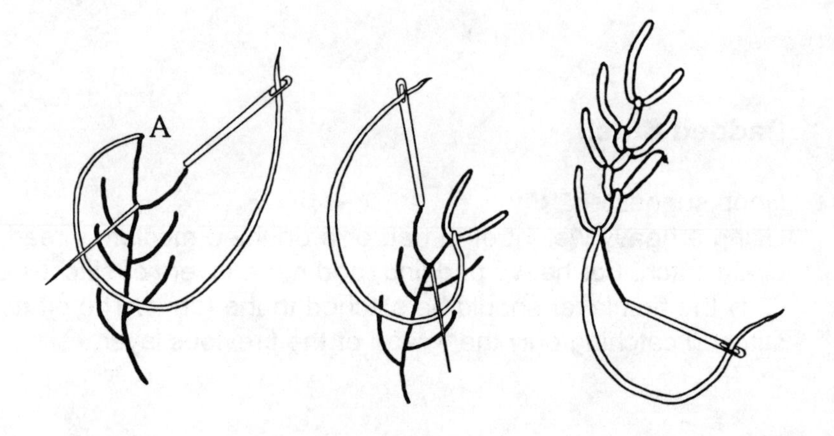

Palestrina Stitch

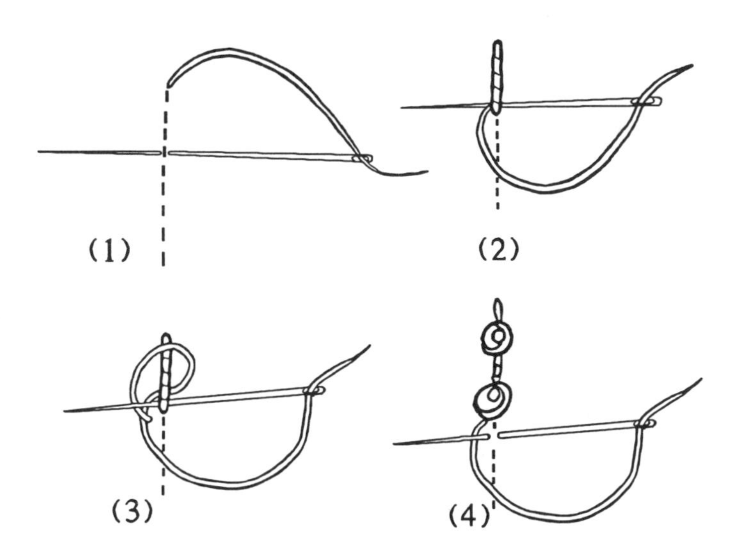

Come up at the beginning of the line and go down about ¼ inch. Catch a very small piece of fabric, then pull through (1).
Loop the thread down to the right and slide the needle under the stitch. Pull it through leaving a small loop (2).
Flip the loop up and slide the needle once more under the stitch without catching the fabric or thread (3). Pull the needle through until a knot is formed (4). Repeat the same steps to form the next knot. Keep the knots about ¼ inch from each other.

Hopper stitch

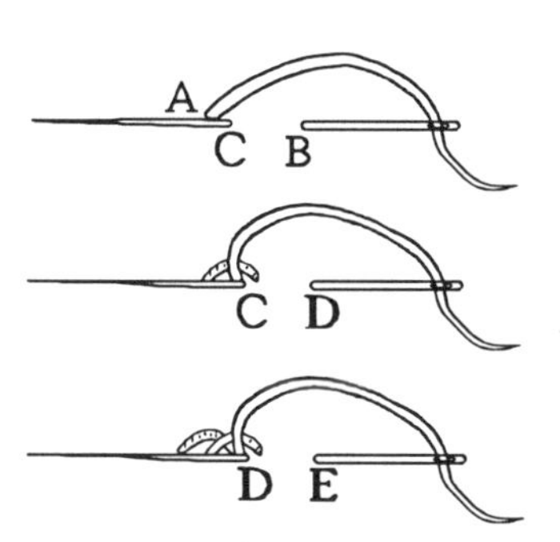

Come up at A and pull through. Insert the needle at B and up at C pulling through. Insert the needle at D and up at C pulling through. Insert the needle at E and up at D pulling through.
Always go down a short distance ahead of the last stitch and up half way on the last stitch.

Spiral Wheel

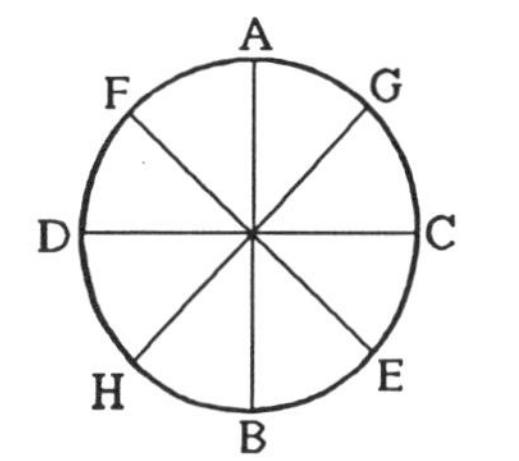

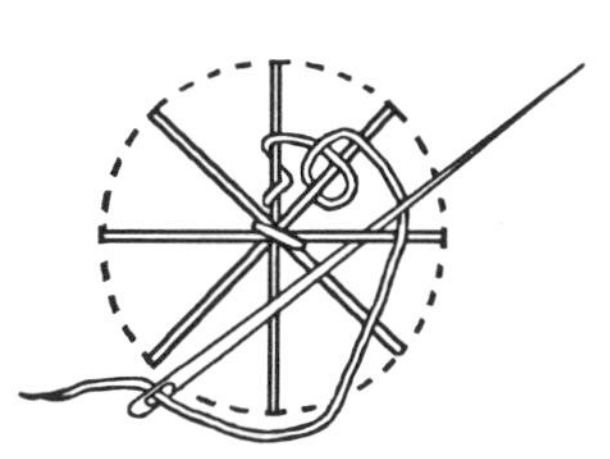

Hoop suggested.
In this example we are using a circle with eight sections but any number, whether even or odd, can be used.
Come up at A and down at B forming a bar. Come up at C, down at D and repeat the steps for E to F and G to H.
Come up in the center on either side of any of the bars and make a small stitch over the bars to tack them down. Come up in the center on the left side of any bar and slide the needle under the same bar right to left. Keeping the thread above and looped over to the right, slide the needle under the bar to the right. Bring each loop against the center. Repeat the steps until the area is filled.

Loop Stitch

Hoop suggested. This stitch can be worked in several different ways*.

1. Make a small bar at the bottom of the petal. Come up on the left side of the bar and insert an empty needle half way through the fabric at the top of the petal. Slide the threaded needle under the bar without catching the fabric. Make the thread go behind the empty needle to form the loop. Repeat as many times is needed.
2. Make two bars on the petal on opposite sides, meeting at the center. Come up at the center and slide the threaded needle under the bars, going around in circles until the desired area is filled.

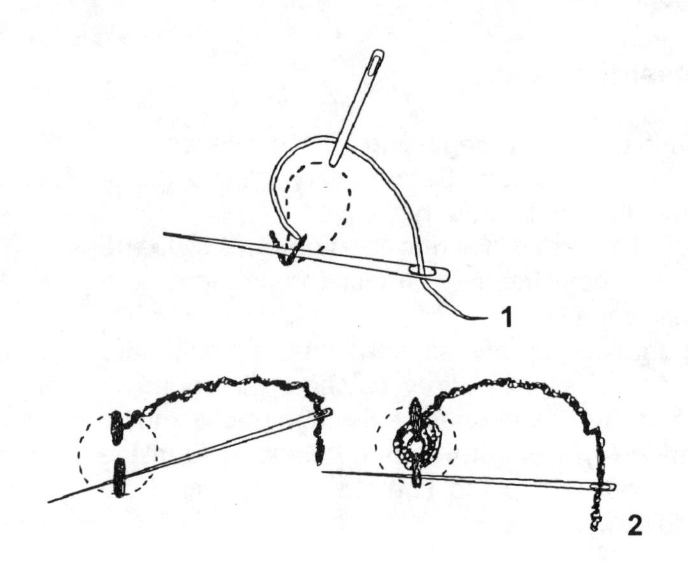

*For an additional variation on the first method, refer to the instructions for Bouclé Rose on page 24.

Regular Leaf

Alternating Satin Stitch

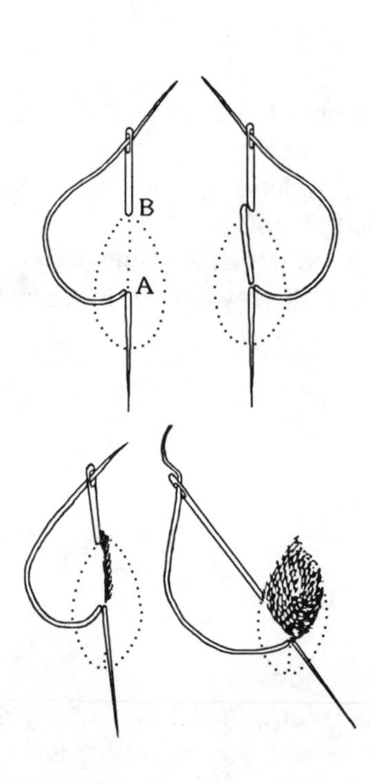

Hoop suggested.
This leaf works best with Iris, Glory and Ciré.
Come up at the tip of the vein at A and pull through. Insert the needle at the tip of the leaf at B and back up at A; pull through. Go down at the tip to the right of the first stitch and come up on the vein below the first stitch and pull through.
Go down again at the tip to the left of the first stitch and come up below the second stitch on the vein. Make the rest of the stitches graduating down alternating from right to left making the stitches very close together. Keep each stitch angled down, not across.

Feather Leaf

Hoop suggested.
This leaf works well with all threads.
Come up at the tip of the leaf at A and pull the thread through. Insert the needle at B and come up in the same hole at A (1). Loop the thread down to the left. Insert the needle at C and come up at D. Keeping the looped thread beneath the needle, pull through (2). Loop the thread to the right and insert the needle at E and come up at F. Pull through with the loop under the needle (3). Keep alternating sides and moving down the vein slightly each time until the area is completed. Make sure your stitches are very close together.

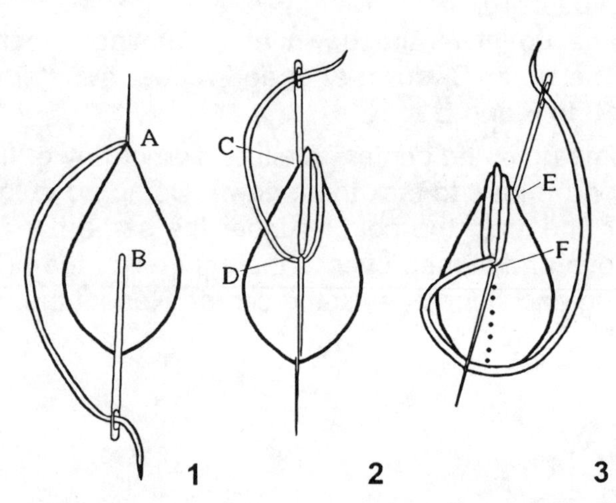

Buttonhole (Blanket) Leaf

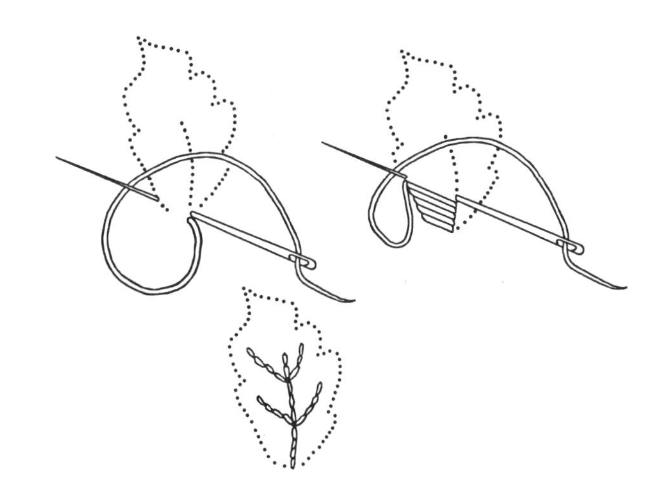

Hoop suggested.
This leaf works well with all threads.
Make close Blanket stitches starting at the bottom of the leaf on the left side. Always go down at the center vein and up at the edge of the leaf. Make the vein in Stem stitch with a lighter colored thread.
To make this leaf thicker and have a ruffled edge, do the first layer in regular Buttonhole (Blanket) Leaf stitch and the second layer in Wrapped Buttonhole stitch.

Single Satin Leaf

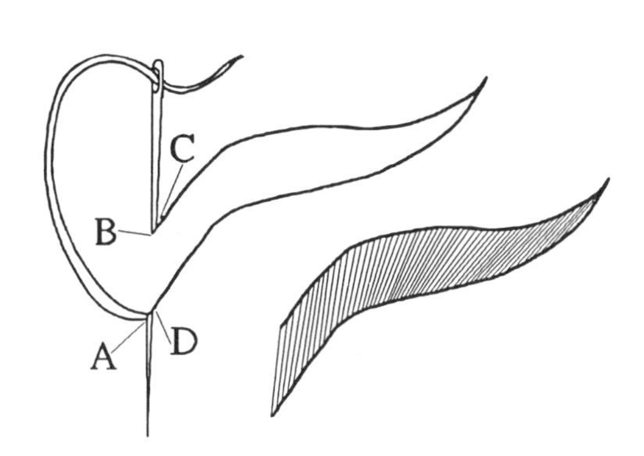

Hoop suggested.
This leaf works best with Iris, Glory and Ciré.
Come up at the bottom of the leaf at A and pull through. Insert the needle at C, go up at D and pull through. Keep a wider space between B and C to keep the stitches at an angle. Do not pull too tight. Continue in the same manner until the tip of the leaf is reached.

Double Sided Satin Leaf

Hoop suggested.
This leaf works best with Iris, Glory and Ciré.
Work the first half of the leaf the same way as the Single Satin Leaf. Stitch the right side following the curves of the leaf. Continue maintaining a slant. The stitches should completely cover the area but do not make them crowded.

Padded Leaf

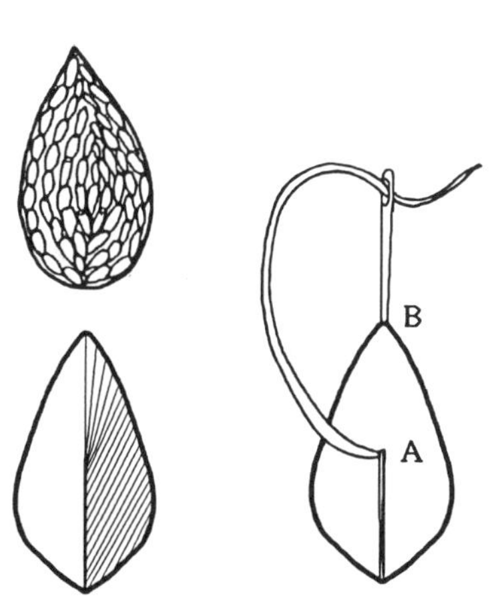

Hoop suggested.
This leaf works best with Iris, Glory or Ciré.
Follow Chain stitch instructions for the padding. Come up at the end of the vein at A. Insert the needle at the tip of the leaf at B and come back up at A. Go down very close to B on the right side and come up slightly below point A on the vein. Continue doing the right side of the leaf. Do the left side following the same steps. By doing it this way, you will obtain a different shading than a regular leaf. Keep the stitches close together.

Cast-on Flower

Lola and Glory - French Knots and Cast-on stitch.

Divide the circle into fifths. Each petal is made with 30 casts. To start the petals, always come up in front of the previous one.
First petal- Come up at A, down at C then up at A without pulling through and cast-on. Pull through and secure at C.
Second petal- Repeat the same procedure going from B to D.
Third petal- Repeat the same procedure going from C to E.
Fourth petal- Repeat the same procedure going from D to A.
Fifth petal- Come up at E, go down behind the first petal at B and come up in front of the petal at E and cast-on.

Center- With Glory thread, fill the center with French Knots.

Buds- Made with two petals. From A to B make ten casts, then from A to C make twelve casts. Using the same thread as the calyx, make two small branches in Couching stitch coming out from the inside of the bud at D.

Calyx- With Iris, make a bullion with twelve wraps from E to F.

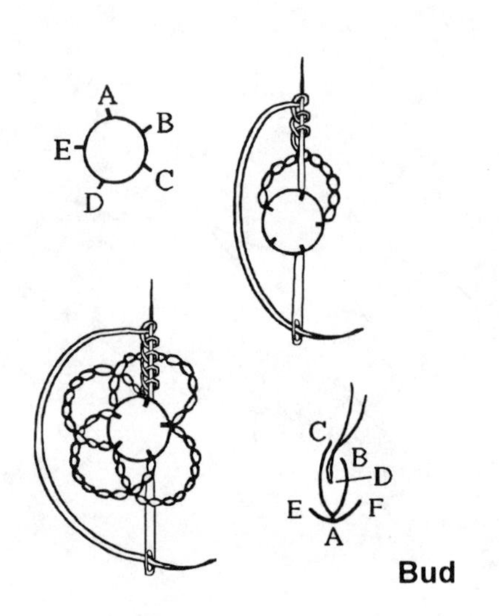

Peach Blossom

Nova and Glory - Detached Buttonhole, French Knots and Straight stitch.

Divide the circle into fourths. Make a small bar from A to B and follow the instructions for detached buttonhole stitch. The first row is done with five loops. For the second row, place two loops on the center loop for a total of six loops. Make the remaining petals the same way; the next from B to C, another from C to D and the last from D to A.

Center- With Glory, make three straight stitches from the center going into the petal to hold it in place. Fill the center with French knots.

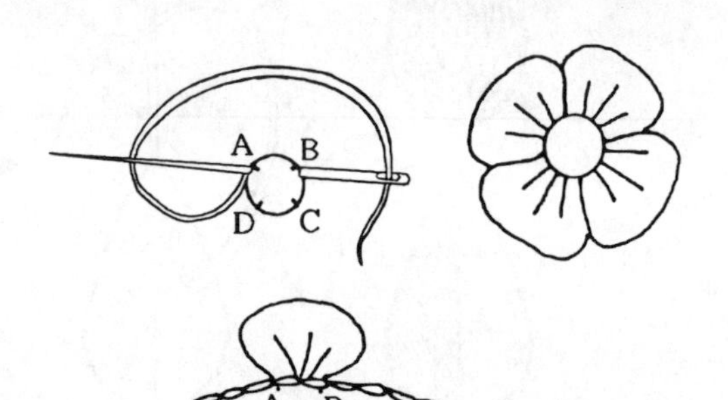

Bud- With the same thread as the flower, make a bar from A to B. Make three loops for the first row, and four loops for the second.

Calyx- Using the same thread as the branches, make three straight stitches into the bud from the base to the middle of the petal.

Geron Daisy

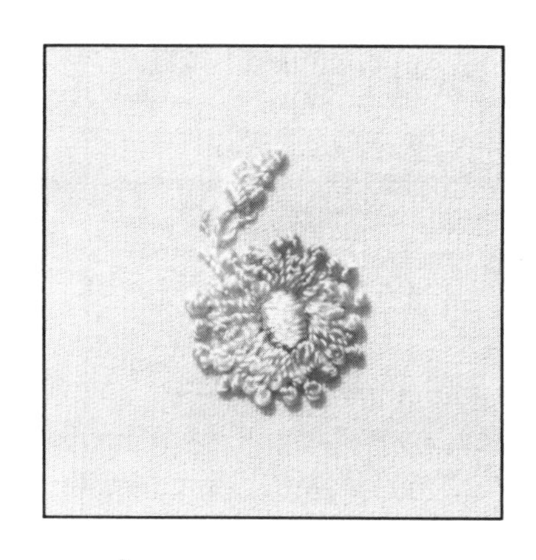

Lola, Glory and Iris - Pistil stitch, French Knots, and Bullion stitch.
Hoop suggested.

Petals- Start at the edge of the circle and radiate outward. Make the pistil stitches very close together with three wraps each.
Alternate lengths all around the circle.

Center- Glory - Fill with French knots or Satin stitch.

Bud- Make the Pistil stitches coming out from the center base of the bud radiating upwards. Make several pistil stitches for each bud.

Calyx- Iris - Make two bullions under the bud from A to B. One with 15 wraps, the bottom one with 12 wraps.

Japanese Violet

Lola - Bullion stitch and French Knots.
Hoop suggested.

Divide the circle into fifths.
<u>Bottom row</u>- Each petal is made with 45 wraps.
First Petal- Make the bullion from A to B anchoring at B.
Second- Make the bullion from E to A anchoring at A.
Third- Make the bullion from D to E anchoring at E.
Fourth- Make the bullion from C to D anchoring at D.
Fifth- Make the bullion from B to C anchoring at C.

<u>Top row</u>- Each petal is made with 40 wraps. Place the petals in between the petals of the first row, using the same procedure as above.

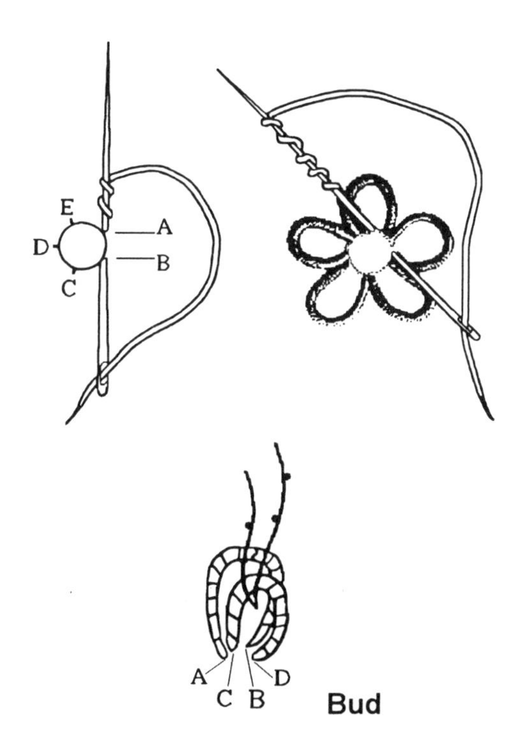

Center- With Glory thread, fill in the center with French Knots.

Bud- From A to B, make a bullion with 40 wraps and anchor at B. From C to D, make another bullion with 35 wraps and anchor at D.

Calyx- Use the same thread as the stems.
Make a 15 wrap bullion from A to D. Make two small branches in couching stitch coming out of the bud.

Bouclé Rose

Bouclé - Loop stitch and Couching .

Come up through the fabric at any dot and go down at the next. Make five bars this way. Come up on the left side of the bar and insert an empty needle half way through the fabric at the top of the petal. Make the thread go behind the empty needle to form the loop. Slide the threaded needle under the bar without catching the fabric (1). Go back around the empty needle in the opposite direction sliding the threaded needle under the bar without catching the fabric (2). Make 8 or 10 loops. Go down at the base of the petal and up inside the loops right in front of the second needle. Hold the petals with one hand and remove the second needle. Go down on the outside of the loops and make a small stitch to secure the petal (3). Do the remaining petals the same way.

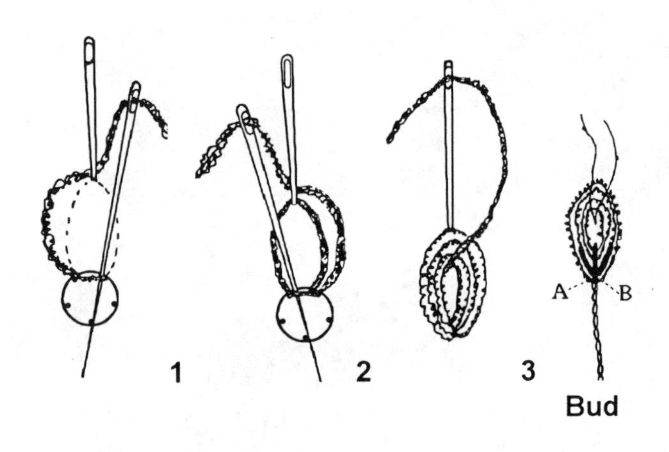

Center- Fill in the center with French Knots.

Bud- Make a single petal with 8 to 10 loops and two small branches in couching stitch coming out of the bud.

Calyx- Use the same thread that was used for the stems. Here are several possibilities.

Make a few straight stitches into the bud from the base.
Make a 15 wrap bullion from point A to B.
Make a cast-on stitch from point A to B with 15 casts, and a second row beneath the first with 10 casts.

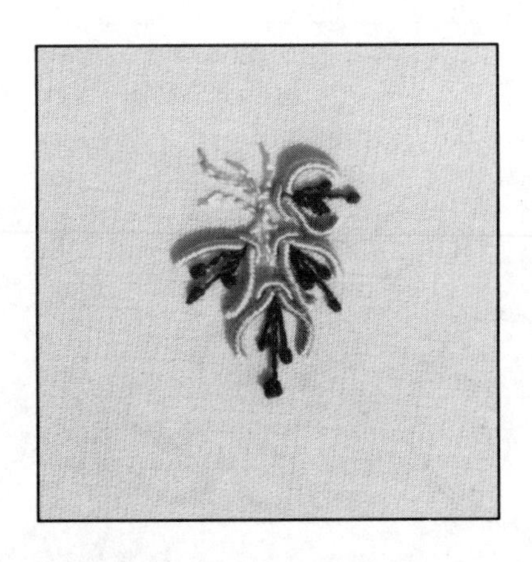

Creeping Flower

Hoop suggested.
Lola - Bullion and Pistil stitch.
Petals- Make a 12 wrap bullion from A to B and secure at B. Make a second petal from B to C.

Pistils- Make three pistil stitches starting inside at the very bottom of the flower.

Calyx- With the same thread as the stems, make a 15 wrap bullion from D to E. Start and end slightly under the petals.

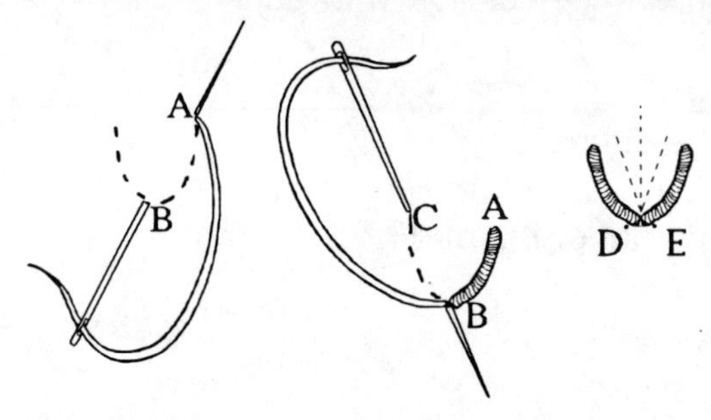

Knotted Lazy Daisy

Lola and Glory - Knotted Lazy Daisy, French Knots and
Bullion stitch.
Hoop suggested.

Petals*- Make a series of knotted lazy daisy stitches with four or five wraps radiating out from the edge of the center. After going down at the tip of a petal, come up at the bottom of the next. For the last petal, go down at the tip and secure.

Center*- With Glory, fill with French knots or satin stitch.

Bud- Make five or six petals with four or five wraps each.

Calyx- With the same thread as the stems, make an 8 wrap bullion starting at C and anchored at D.

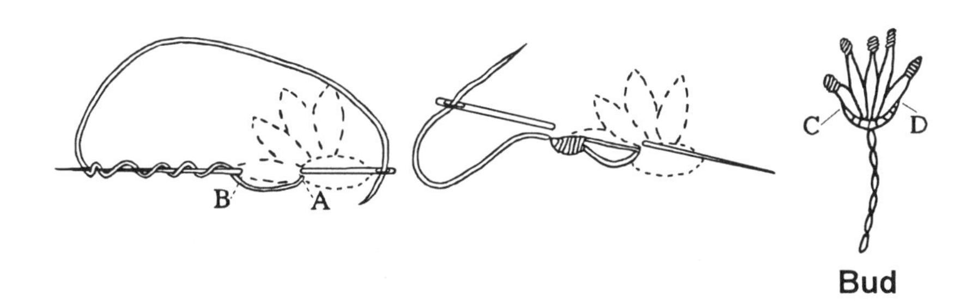

*If you fill the center with satin stitch, fill the center before making the petals.

Rolled Rose

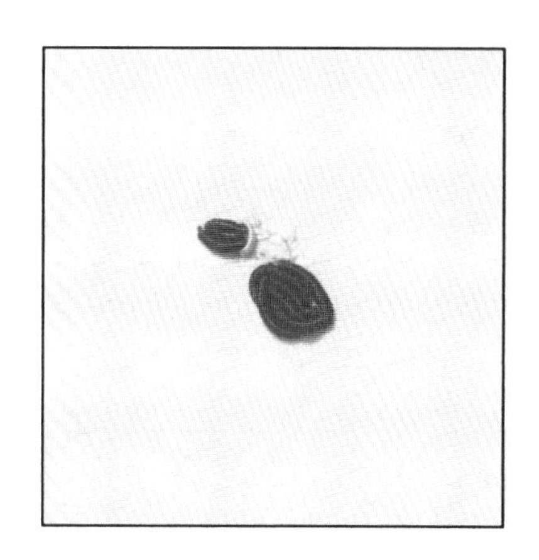

Hoop suggested
Lola - Bullion stitch.
Petals- Start by making two 10 wrap bullions side by side. Follow the diagram for where to place the next four bullion with the following number of wraps. A-B, 12; C-D, 15; E-F, 15 and G-H, 18. Be sure to start and tuck each bullion slightly under the previous one and hide the ends.

Bud- Make two 10 wrap bullions side by side. At the tip, make two small branches coming out from inside the bud. Use the same thread as used for the branches.

Calyx- With the same thread as the stems, make an 8 wrap bullion from A to B. Start slightly underneath one side of the bud and anchor it on the other side.

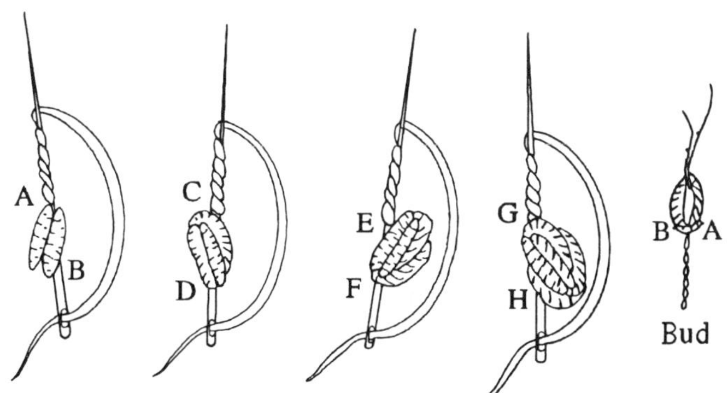

Bullion Rose

Lola - Bullion stitch.

Petals- With Lola thread, do the following;
First row- Divide the circle into fourths. Make 4 bullion with 10 wraps each going from A to B, slightly behind B to C, slightly behind C to D and again slightly behind D to slightly in front of the A Bullion.

Each bullion starts behind and slightly underneath the last one made. Doing this will make the rose stand up.

Second row- 5th Bullion. Make each Bullion in this row with 12 wraps. Start slightly behind the 4th Bullion and anchor behind the next.

Third row- Make each Bullion with 14 wraps. Start slightly behind the last Bullion made in the 2nd row. Anchor behind the next Bullion.

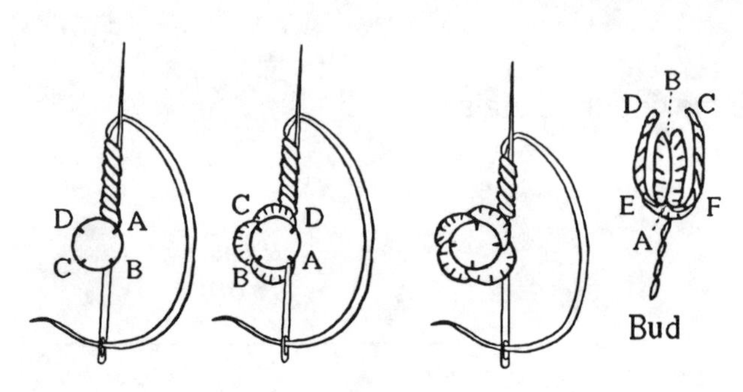

Fourth row- Make each Bullion with 16 wraps. Continue with the same placing procedures.
For a larger rose, add more rows adding 3 to 4 wraps for each Bullion per row.

Bud- From A to B, make two Bullions side by side with 8 wraps each. From A to C, make a Bullion with 15 wraps and then from A to D, 12 wraps.

Calyx- With the same thread as the stems, make a Bullion from E to F with 10 wraps.

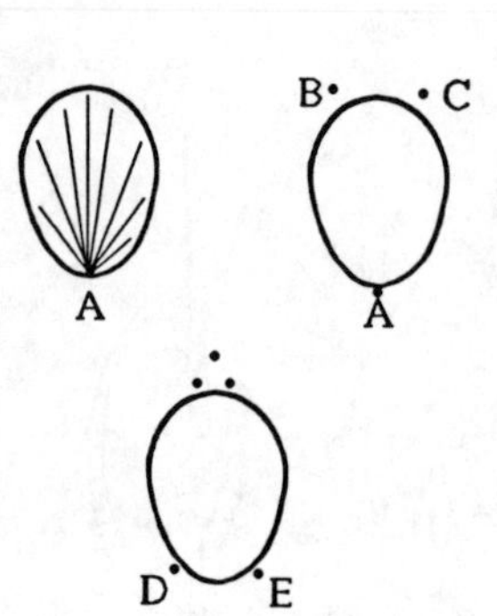

Alpine Bilberry

Iris and Glory - French Knots, Straight, Blanket, and Bullions stitches.

With Iris, come up through the fabric at A and make 8 to 10 Straight stitches into the petal.
Come up again at A and make Blanket stitches over the Straight stitches following the curve of the petal. With Glory, make one Bullion on each side with 25 wraps each from A to B and from A to C.

Center- With Glory thread, make 3 French Knots in a triangle position on the top edge of the flower.

Calyx- With Glory thread, make a 10 wrap Bullion from E to D.

Maria's Rose

Lola - Cast-on and Bullion stitch.

First Petal- Come up at A. Insert the needle at B then up at A; Cast-on 6 times and secure at B.
ALL PETALS SHOULD START SLIGHTLY BEHIND THE LAST ONE.
Second Petal- Come up slightly behind and slightly before B. Insert the needle at C, then up where the thread is coming out. Cast-on 8 times and secure at C.
Third Petal- Come up slightly behind C and insert the needle at D. Come up where the thread is coming out and Cast-on 10 times.
Fourth Petal- Come up slightly behind D and insert the needle just past A, Cast-on 12 times.
Second row- Start behind and in the middle of the previous petal and anchor behind the next petal. In the second row, make 14 Cast-ons per petal. For a larger rose, make more rows of petals and add 2 stitches per petal for each row.

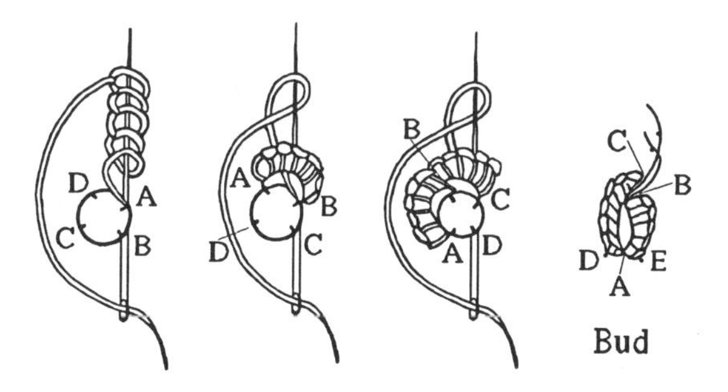

Bud- From A to B, make 10 Cast-ons. From A to C, make 12 Cast-ons. Using the same thread as the calyx, make two small branches in Couching stitch coming out from inside the bud and between the petals.

Calyx- A 12 wrap Bullion under the bud from D to E.

Wild Rose

Nova and Iris - Bullion French Knots and Loop stitch.

Petals- With Iris thread, make two Bullions side by side with 18 wraps each from A to B. Make 5 sets of Bullions this way. Using Nova thread, make one small straight stitch on each petal from A to the inner dot. Starting from the left side of any straight stitch to the outer dot, make 5 or 6 clockwise loops following the loop stitch directions. Continue working on each petal to the left of the one you just did. Using the same thread as the loops, come up through the middle of the Straight stitch and make a French Knot with 3 wraps. On both sides of the Straight stitch make another French Knot with 3 wraps.

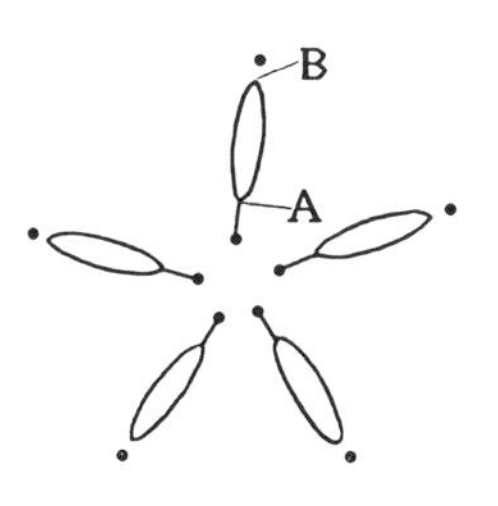

Center- With Iris thread, fill with French Knots with 3 wraps each.

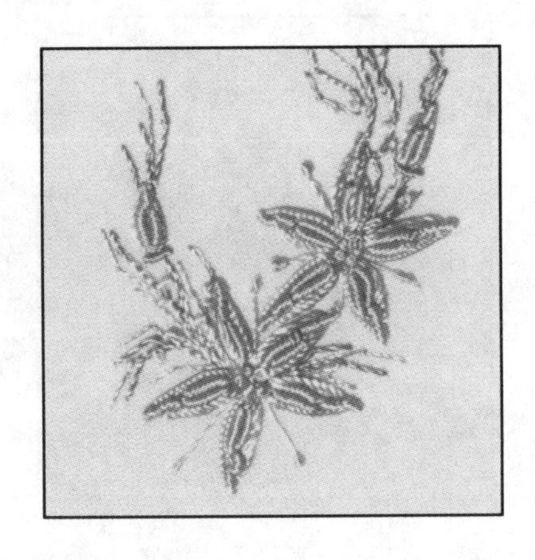

Fancy Daisy

Lola and Glory - Bullion stitch, Knotted Lazy Daisy, French Knots, Pistil and Couching stitches.

Petals- Come up at any dot. Make 2 Bullions side by side from A to B with 8 wraps each. Come up at A and make a Knotted Lazy Daisy stitch to C with 3 wraps. Again, come up at A and make another Knotted Lazy Daisy stitch to D with 3 wraps. Repeat the steps for the remaining petals.

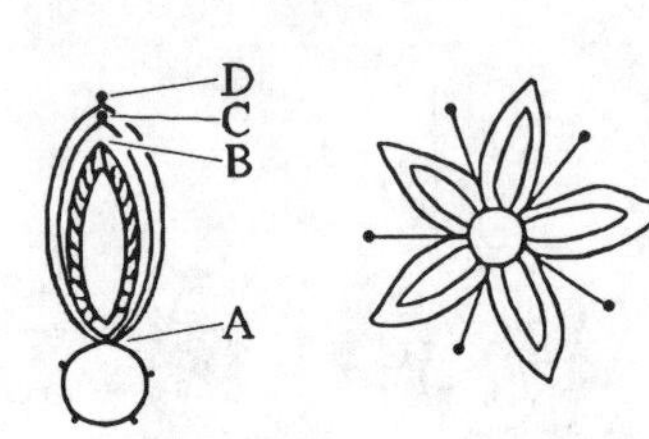

E F
Bud

Center- Using Glory, come up in between the petals and make a Pistil stitch the same length as the petals with 4 raps each. Fill the center with French Knots.

Bud- Come up at the tip of the stem and make one petal the same way as the main flower.

Calyx- 10 wrap bullion from E to F.

Cast-on Daisy

Lola and Iris - Cast-on and French Knot stitch.
Hoop suggested

Petals- Come up along the circle on any petal and insert the needle where the tip of the petal will be. Come up where the thread is coming out and Cast-on 12 times. Pull the needle through the Cast-on. Go down at the tip and come up at the bottom of the next petal. Make all remaining petals the same way.

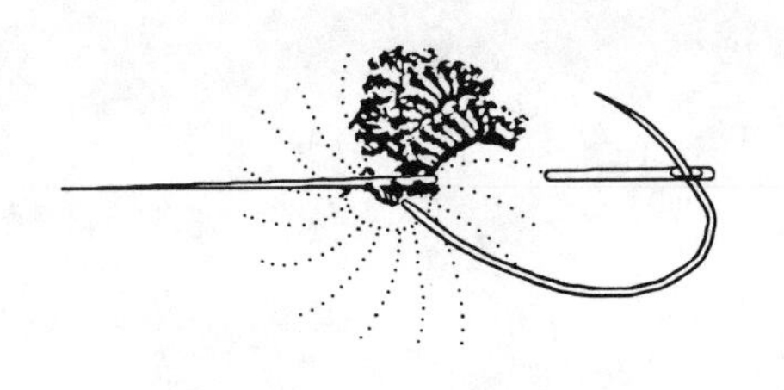

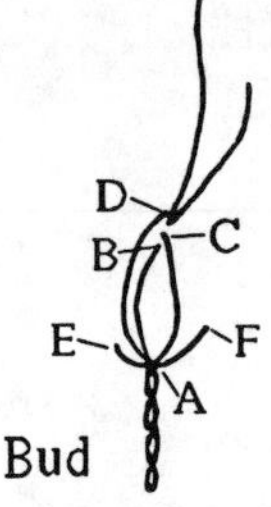

Center- With Iris, fill the circle with French Knots.

Bud- Using same thread as the flower, make three petals starting at A. From A to B, 8 Cast-ons; to C, 12 Cast-ons and to D, 15 Cast-ons. From the tip, make two branches with the same thread as the calyx.

Calyx- Make 12 Cast-ons from E to F

African Daisy

Hoop suggested.
Lola and Nova - Double Cast-on, Knotted Lazy Daisy, Bullion, and Turkey stitch.

Petals- Use Lola thread.
All petals start at the base. Come up just to the left side of the center vein. Make a series of knotted lazy daisy stitches going from the vein to the edge of the petal wrapping the thread five times for each. Make the stitches very close together and slanting upward. At the tip, make three stitches into the same hole and then continue going down the right side of petal. Make all of the petals the same way.

Veins- Use Nova thread and prepare to make a double cast-on stitch. Come up at C, insert the needle at D and then come back up at C. Make a double cast-on with 15 casts on each side. Go down at D to secure.

Center- With Lola, fill the circle with Turkey stitches made very close together.

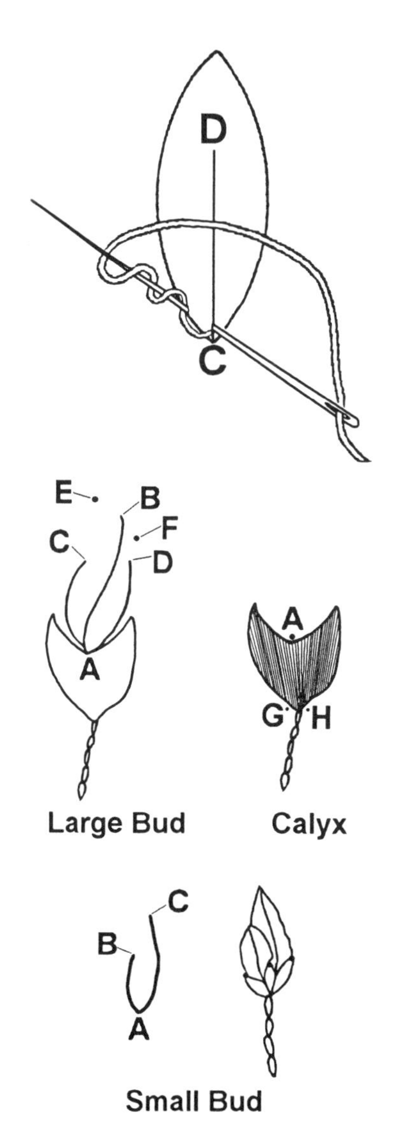

Large Bud- With Lola thread, make one double cast-on stitch from A to B with 30 casts. Make one petal from A to C and another from A to D. Make the petals with 16 casts each. With Iris thread, starting behind the center petal at A, make one bullion from A to E with 50 wraps and another from A to F with 40 wraps.

Calyx- Iris - Straight stitch and Detached Bullion stitch.
Come up at the base of the calyx right at the end of the stem. Fill the area with straight stitches made very close together. Make a bar from G to H. Come up on the G side below the bar and place three detached bullions with five wraps each on the bar. Secure at H. Come up at G again to add another row.
Make two detached bullion stitches on the first bullion, one on the second and two on the third. Continue adding rows until you reach the bottom of the petals. For each row, always make two detached bullions onto the first and last bullions of the previous row and one on all the rest. When you reach point A, make only the first two detached bullions. Go under the rest of the row and make the last two. Then make one detached bullion on each side to form a **V**. Tack down the sides with small stitches.

Small Bud- Lola - Double Cast-on stitch and Lazy Daisy stitch.
Make two petals, the first from A to B with 8 double casts, the second from A to C with 12 double casts.

Calyx- With Lola thread, place three lazy daisy stitches from the end of the stem going over the petals.

Picotee Dahlia

Lola and Iris - Cloth floral wire - Detached Buttonhole, Detached Bullion, Straight stitch, Knotted Lazy Daisy, Spiral Wheel and French Knots.

This flower has the same basic petals as the Crown Dahlia.

Bottom petals. Make a bar from A to B and follow the instructions for detached buttonhole stitch. Make the rows following the chart at right for the number of loops. Always add or subtract loops on the edges. At the tip, when only one stitch remains, go with the needle and thread behind the petal and weave the thread to the base of the petal.

Make a bar from B to C and work the second petal the same way as the first. The remaining petals go from C to D; D to E; E to F and the last one from F to A.

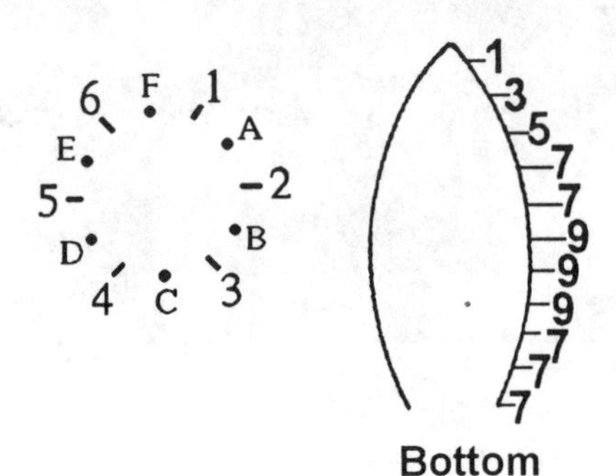

Bottom petal

After the six petals are done, thread a new strand of the same thread and come up from the bottom at the base of the left side of any petal. Pull the thread through and insert the needle through the edge of the first loop without catching the fabric. Make a detached bullion stitch with six wraps. Pull the bullion smooth and tight. Continue making detached bullions with six wraps each along the edge until you reach the tip of the petal. At the very tip, make one with 8 wraps. Now come down on the right side of the petal making the stitches with six wraps each. At the end, go down and secure. Make all the petals the same way.

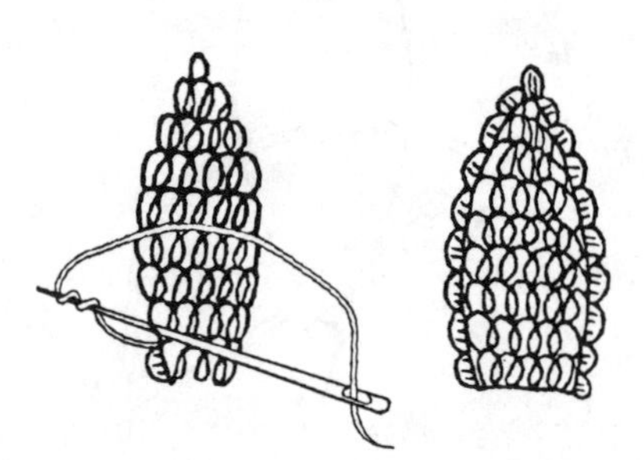

With cloth floral wire, come up through the fabric at the bottom and behind any petal and lay the wire around the back of the petal. Using the same thread as the petals, make couching stitches to hold the wire in place.

Top Petals. Use Lola thread. It can be the same color as the bottom petals or another color or shade for contrast. Come up right in front of a bottom petal. Make a bar from 1 to 2 and stitch the same way as the bottom petals following the chart for top petals. Do the remaining petals from 2 to 3; 3 to 4; 4 to 5; 5 to 6 and 6 to 1.

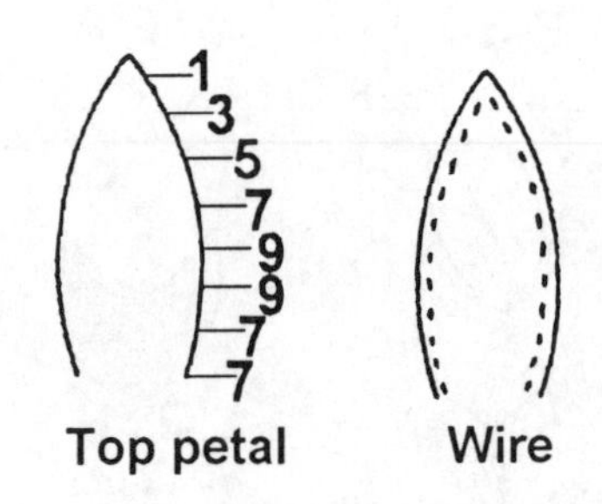

Top petal Wire

Center- Using Iris thread, make the center following the instructions for making a spiral wheel.

Large Bud- Use the same thread as the flower. Make a bar from A to B and make one petal the same way as the top petals. Make another bar from A to B and make a second petal over the first one. Wire the same way as the flower.

Calyx- Using the same thread as the stems, make straight stitches coming from the stem to 1/4 of the way into the petals.

Small Bud- Same thread as the flowers. Make knotted lazy daisy stitches with three wraps each. All stitches start at the bottom at A to the tip of the bullion. First make the longer ones, then the short ones over them.

Calyx- With the same thread as the stems, start at A and make a few lazy daisy stitches into the bud.

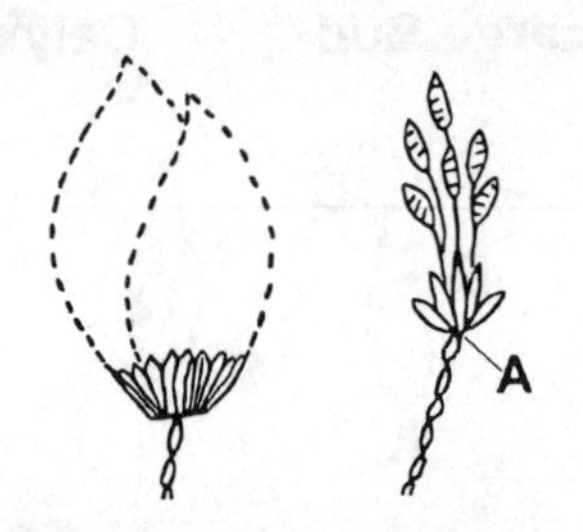

Large bud Small bud

Crown Dahlia

Lola, Iris and Glory - Detached Buttonhole, French Knot, and Straight stitch.

This flower has the same basic petals as the Picotee.
Bottom petals. Using Lola thread, work on the bottom petals first. Make a bar from A to B. Follow instructions for detached buttonhole stitch and make the rows following the chart to the right for the number of loops. Always add or subtract loops at the edges. After doing the last stitch at the tip, go with the needle down at the **X**. Pull the thread through and secure. Start each petal with a new strand of thread. Do the remaining petals from B to C; C to D; D to E; E to F and F to A. Make all the petals the same way.

Top Petals. Use Lola thread. It can be the same color as the bottom petals or another color or shade for contrast. Come up right in front of a bottom petal. Make a bar from 1 to 2 and stitch the same way as the bottom petals following the chart for top petals securing at the tip. Do the remaining petals from 2 to 3; 3 to 4; 4 to 5; 5 to 6 and 6 to 1.

Center- With Iris thread, make sraight stitches from the edge of the small circle to the petals very close together. Make another layer over the first one. With a contrasting color, start in the center of the small circle and make a few straight stitches over the first ones. Fill in the center with French knots.

Bud- Make the bar from A to B and make one petal the same way as a top petal.

Calyx- Using the same thread as used for the stems, make straight stitches from the end of the stem to 1/4 of the way into the petal making the stitches different lengths.

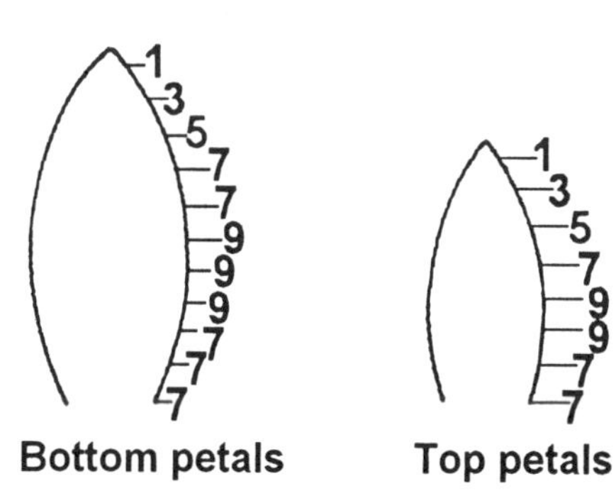

Bottom petals **Top petals**

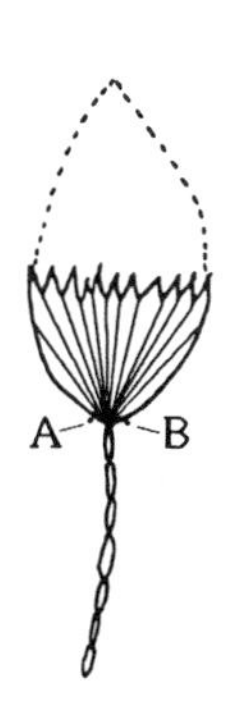

Bud

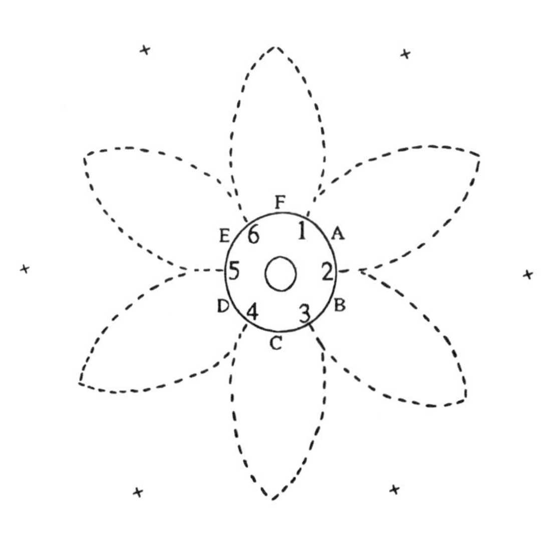

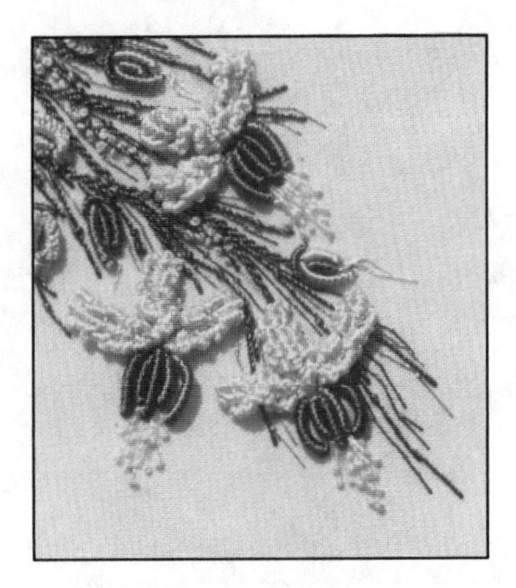

Petite Fuchsia

Lola, Nova and Glory - Knotted Double Cast-on, Bullion and Pistil stitch.

Petals- With Lola thread, make a knotted double cast-on stitch for each petal. Go from A to each tip. Each is made with 24 casts; 12 on each side of the needle.

Cup- With Nova thread starting at A, make a bullion stitch to B with 12 wraps, from A to C with 10 wraps, and from A to D with 15.
Repeat C and D on the other side.

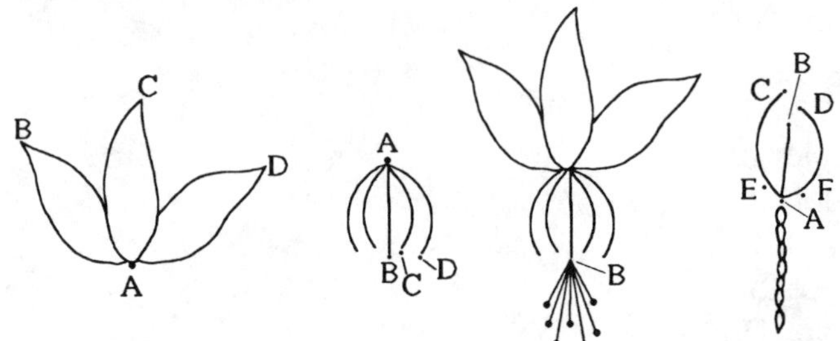

Bud

Pistils- With Glory thread, make pistil stitches with three wraps each coming out from the end of the center bullion.

Bud- With Nova thread, start at A and make a bullion stitch to B with five wraps, to C with eight wraps and to D with ten wraps.

Calyx- With the same thread as the stems, make a bullion from E to F with eight wraps.

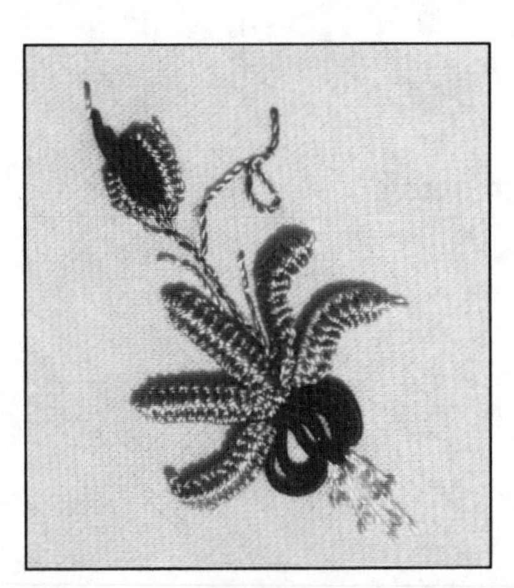

Ashah Fuchsia

Lola, Iris and Glory - Double Cast-on, Bullion, Pistil and Straight stitch.

Petals- With Lola thread, make double cast-on stitches for all five petals. Start at A and go to the tip. Do each with 24 casts; 12 on each side of the needle.

Cup- With Lola thread, make a bullions from A to B with 15 wraps, from A to C with 12 wraps, from A to D with 15 wraps, and from A to E with 18 wraps. Repeat C, D, & E on the other side.

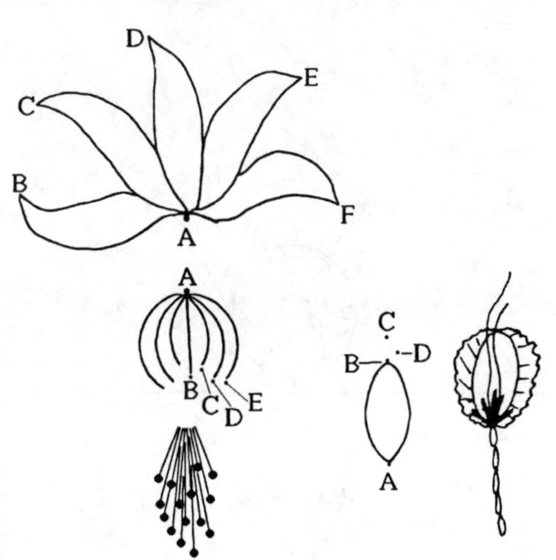

Bud

Pistils- With Glory thread, make pistil stitches with three wraps each coming out from the end of the center bullions.

Bud- With Iris thread, fill the center area with straight stitches coming out from A . Make them close together.
Make a cast-on stitch on both sides of the straight stitches from A to B, each one with 12 casts. Make two bullions over the straight stitches. From A to D with 15 wraps and from A to C with 20 wraps.

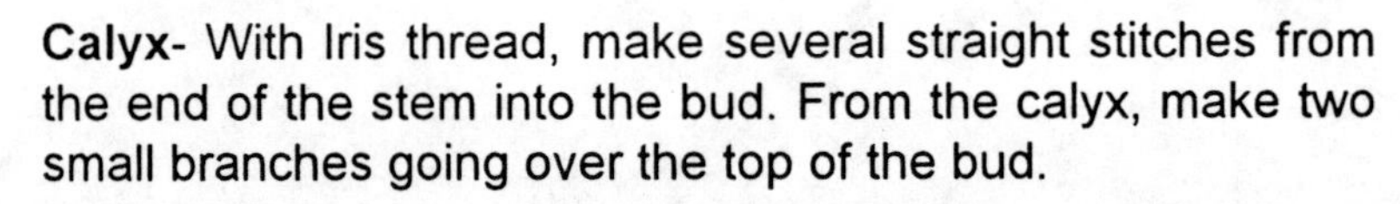

Calyx- With Iris thread, make several straight stitches from the end of the stem into the bud. From the calyx, make two small branches going over the top of the bud.

Sonata Fuchsia

Iris, Lola and Glory - Bullion, Knotted Lazy Daisy, Cast-on and Pistil stitch. Hoop suggested.

Petals- Iris thread. All petals start at the base.
Come up just to the left side of the center vein. Make a series of knotted lazy daisy stitches going from the vein to the edge of the petal wrapping the thread six times for each. Make the stitches very close together and slanting upward. At the tip, make three stitches into the same hole and then continue going down the right side of petal. Make all of the petals the same way.

Veins- With Lola thread, come up at the tip of the vein, insert the needle at the base of the petal and up at the tip where the thread is coming out. Make a bullion stitch with 50 wraps and anchor at the tip. Make all of the veins the same way.

Inner Cup- With Lola thread, Make a bullion with 20 wraps from the center of the flower to the tip of the center line, point A. Make two more bullions, one on each side of the first with 18 wraps each.

Outer Cup- With Lola thread, make a cast-on stitch with 16 casts going from A to B. Anchor at B. Next, cast 26 times from A to C. Anchor at C. Cast 18 times from A to D & 26 times from A to E.

Pistils- Using Glory thread, come up at the end of the center bullion of the inner cup, and make three pistil stitches wrapping each one five times and anchored at each dot.

Petals

Veins

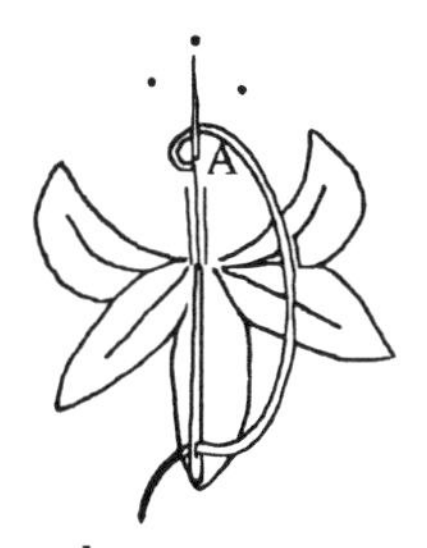

Inner cup

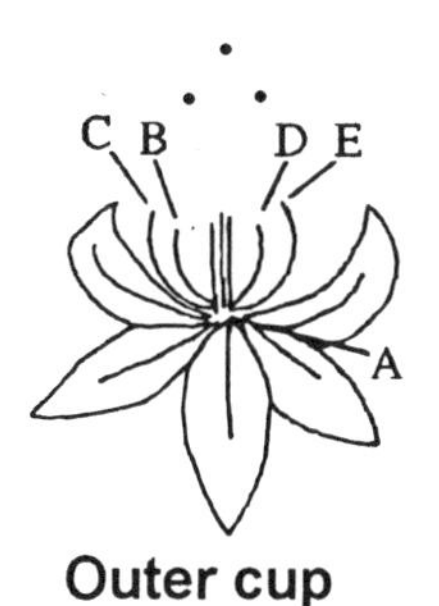

Outer cup

Eucalyptus Flower

Lola - Bullion and Pistil stitch.

Petals- Make the first two bullions with ten wraps each and the remaining bullions with 15 wraps. Make the bullions in numerical order following the placement on the diagram.

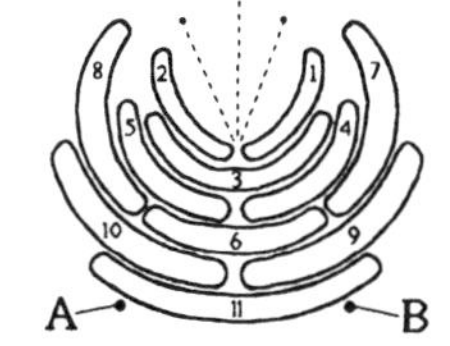

Pistils- Make three pistil stitches between petals 1 & 2.

Calyx- With the same thread as used for the stems, make a bullion from A to B with 12 wraps.

Columbine

Iris and Glory - Padded stitch, Satin stitch, Bullion and French Knots. Hoop suggested.

Petals- Thread two strands of Iris together. Come up on the edge of the circle and make three layers of padded stitch in a spiral pattern filling the area of the flower.
With one strand of Iris, make straight stitches very close together over the padding starting on the edge of the circle and going to the edge of the petal.
Make a bullion from A to B with 30 wraps and repeat for each petal.
With Glory thread, come up at the base of each petal and make a bullion with 25 wraps along its center not quite reaching the edge. Make another bullion on each side of the center one with 20 wraps each.

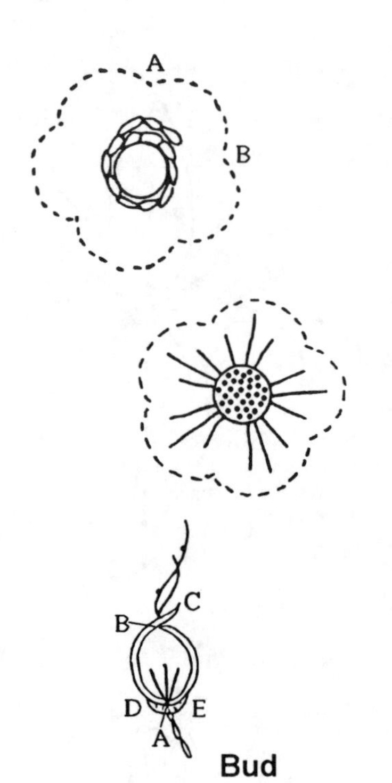

Center- Glory thread. Fill in the remaining space with French knots.

Bud- Fill the area with padded stitch. Make the straight stitches over the padding come out from point A and radiate to the top. With the same thread as the center, make three bullions into the bud from point A. Make the center one with 12 wraps and the side ones with 8 wraps each. Using the same thread as the petals, make a 30 wrap bullion from A to B and a 35 wrap bullion from A to C. Using the same thread as the calyx, make two small branches in couching stitch coming out from the top of the bud.

Calyx- With Iris thread, make one bullion with 8 wraps from D to E.

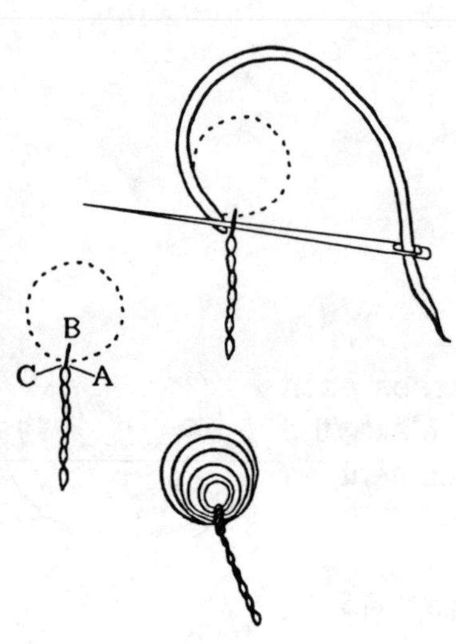

Mini Blossom

Nova - Loop and Bullion stitch.

With the same thread as used for the stems, make a bullion from A to B with 8 wraps. With Nova thread, come up through the material on the left side of the bullion at C. Loop the thread from left to right and slide the threaded needle under the bullion. Make the first loop the same size as the circle. Make all the others decreasing in size. Go down under the bullion and secure the thread when done.

Blanket Bud

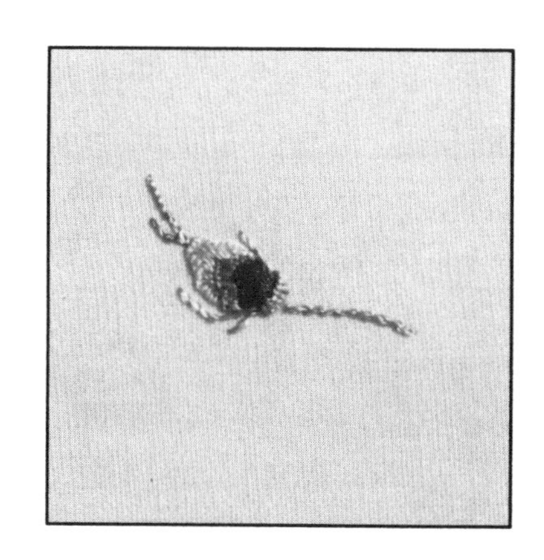

Glory - Buttonhole and Cast-on stitch.
Hoop suggested.

All stitches for this bud come out from point A. Using a light color, make buttonhole stitches over the whole bud (1). Using a medium color, make buttonhole stitches again over half of the bud (2). Using a dark color, make buttonhole stitches over half of the medium color (3).

Calyx- With the same thread as the stems, make a cast-on stitch from B to C with eight casts. Make small branches in couching stitch from the tip and sides of the bud.

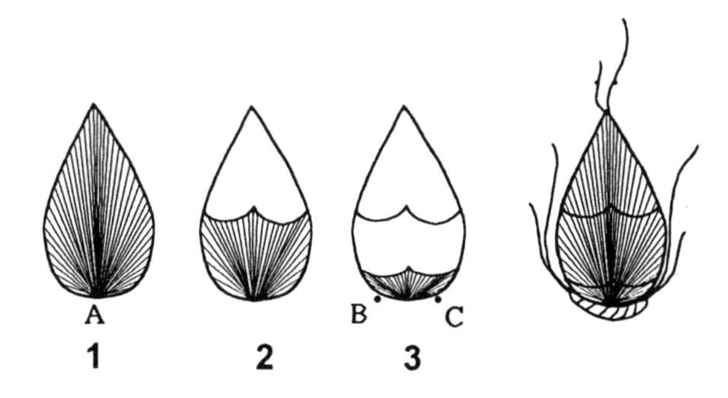

Thrift Flower

Glory - Bullion, Cast-on and Pistil stitch

Make a ten wrap bullion from A to B, and another from A to C.
Come up at A and take a very small bite of fabric to the right. Make a bullion with 40 wraps. Make a second bullion to the left the same way. Come up between the two bullions at the top and make three pistil stitches with two wraps each.

Calyx- With the same thread as the fine growth, make a cast-on stitch from E to F with 15 casts.

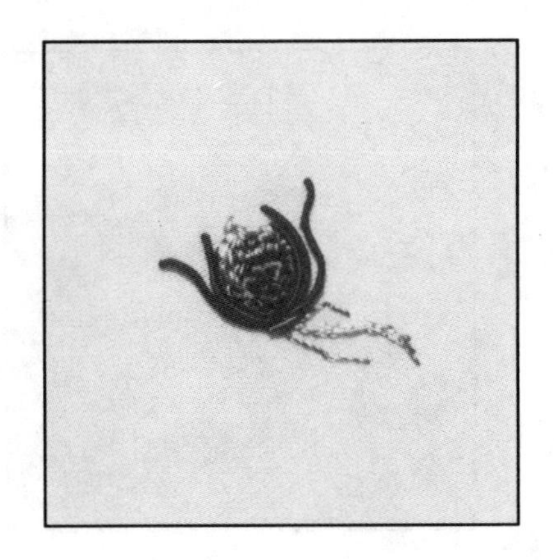

Spider Flower

Nova and Lola - Detached Buttonhole and Bullion stitch.

Petals- Using Nova thread, make a small bar at the base of the flower from A to B. Place 3 loops on the bar. The next three rows have five loops each. The 4th row has three loops and the 5th has one loop in the middle.
With Lola thread, come up at C. Make 6 Bullions; each one starting at C. From C to D, 25 wraps; to E, 25 wraps; to F, 35 wraps; to G, 35 wraps; to H, 40 wraps and to I, 40 wraps.

Calyx- Using the same thread as the stems, make a Bullion from J to K with 12 wraps.

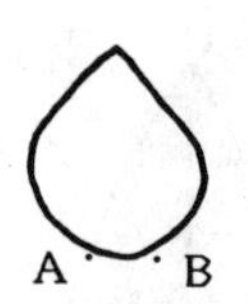

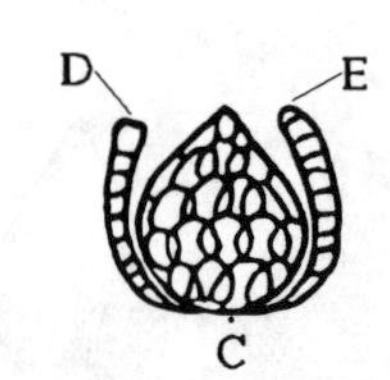

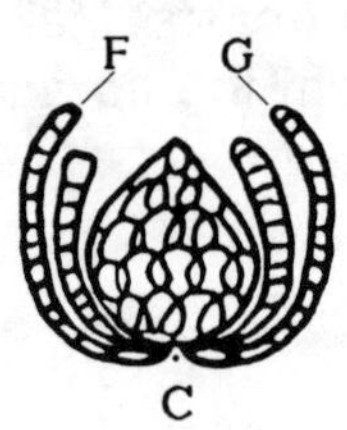

Snowbells

Bouclé and Glory - Loop stitch, Pistil and Bullion stitch.

Thread Bouclé on a darning needle and come up through the fabric at the base of the flower. Make 2 small bars in a V shape into the petals. Come up through the fabric on the left side of one of the bars. Place a second needle at the tip of the petal. With the threaded needle, go under the bar and around the second needle. Repeat 6 or 8 times until the petal is filled. Go down at the bottom of the petal and come up at the tip in front of the second needle. Make a Straight stitch over the loops to secure. Do the second petal the same way.

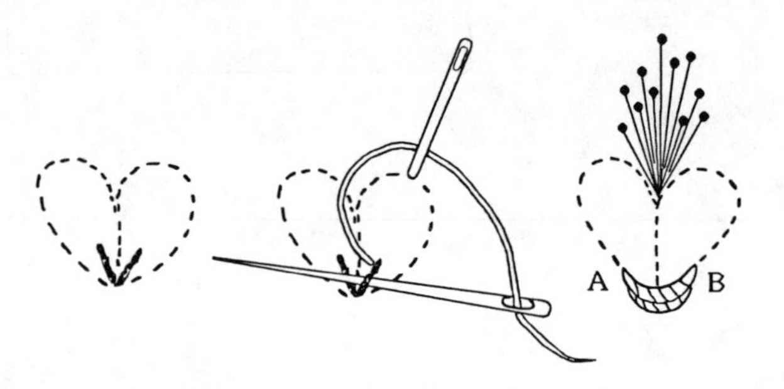

Pistil- With Glory, make several Pistil stitches with 3 wraps each coming out from the center of the flower.

Calyx- Made with the same thread as the stems by making two Bullions from A to B. The top one with 20 wraps and the bottom one with 15 wraps.

Baby's Breath

Glory

Baby's Breath are small flowers that add to and enhance any design.

1- Lazy Daisy stitch, 6 petals starting from the center.
2- Knotted Lazy Daisy stitch, 6 petals starting from the center.
3- Cast-on stitch, 3 petals with 10 stitches each. Work them from A to B, B to C and C to A.
4- Bullion stitch, 8 petals starting from the center with 10 wraps each.
5- Bullion stitch, 4 petals with 20 wraps each. From A to B, B to C,
C to D and D to A.
6- Pistil stitch, starting from the center; 8 petals with 3 wraps each.

Centers- Each flower has one French Knot in the middle.

Berry Flower

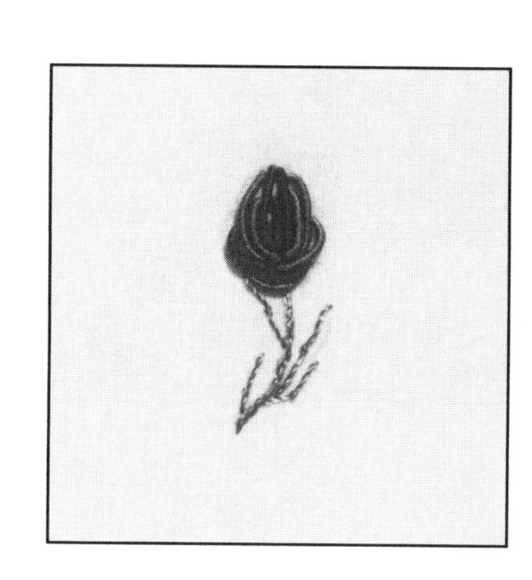

Lola - Bullion stitch.

Come up at the base of the flower at A and make a 15 wrap Bullion to B.
From A to C, make a 22 wrap Bullion on each side.
From A to D, make a 12 wrap Bullion on each side.
From A to E, make a 15 wrap Bullion on each side.
From A to F, make an 8 wrap Bullion on each side.
From G to H make a 10 wrap Bullion.

Calyx- Using the same thread as the stem, make an 8 wrap Bullion from I to J.

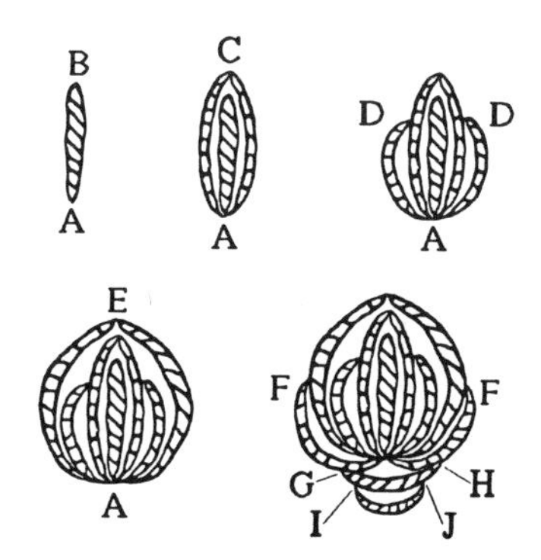

French Hydrangea

Glory - French Knots, Buttonhole, Bullion, and Lazy Daisy stitch.

Petals- Come up on the edge of the center circle. Make the Buttonhole stitches to the flower's edge very close together. With a contrasting color, make 4 Bullions with 35 wraps each stitching clockwise. The first Bullion extends from A to C. The second one from B to D going over the second. The fourth goes from D to B passing over the third Bullion and under the first.

Center- Fill in with French Knots.

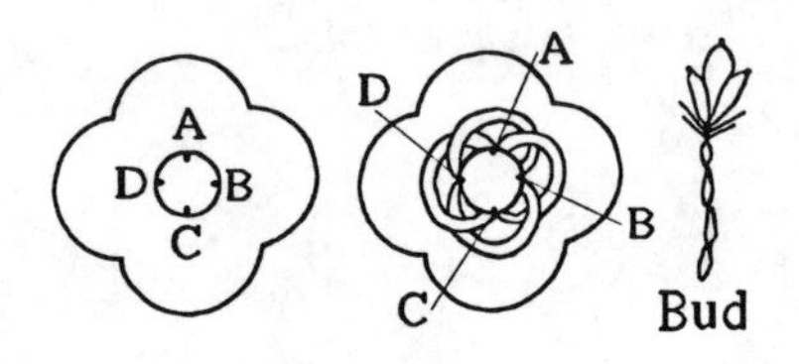

Bud- Using the same thread as the petals; make 3 Lazy Daisy stitches starting from the bottom. The center one should be longer than the others.

Calyx- With the same thread as used for the stems, make two Straight stitches on each side.

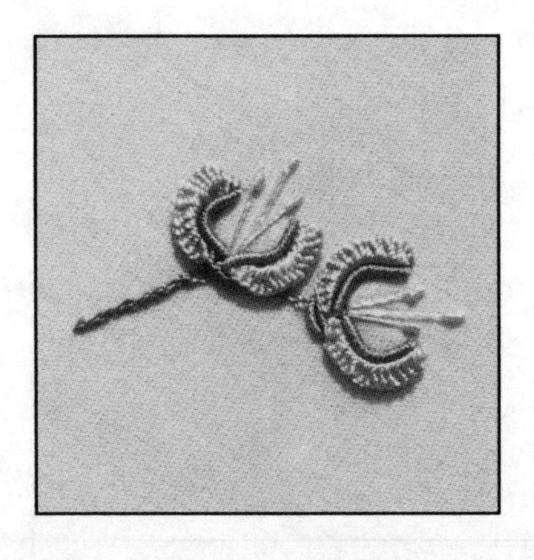

Jasmine

Lola and Glory - Bullion, Cast-on and Pistil stitch.

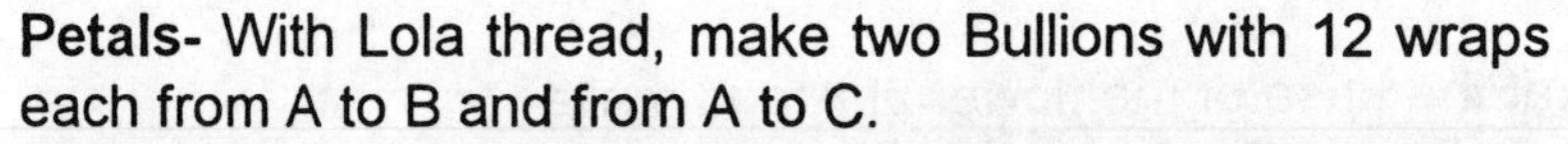
Petals- With Lola thread, make two Bullions with 12 wraps each from A to B and from A to C.
On the outer side of each Bullion, make a Cast-on with 12 wraps.

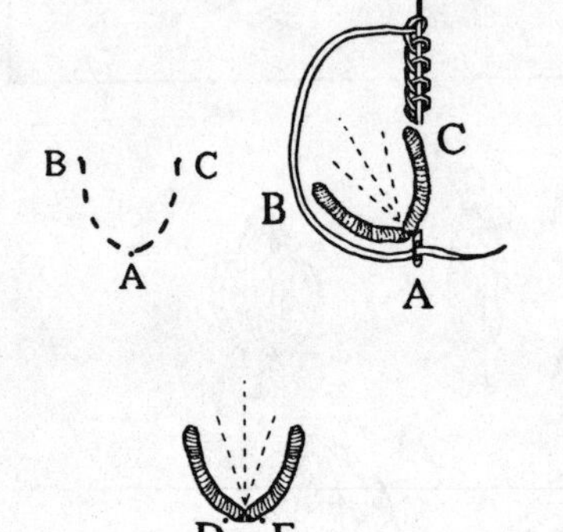

Pistils- With Glory thread, start inside at the very bottom of the flower and make 3 Pistils stitches with 3 to 4 wraps each.

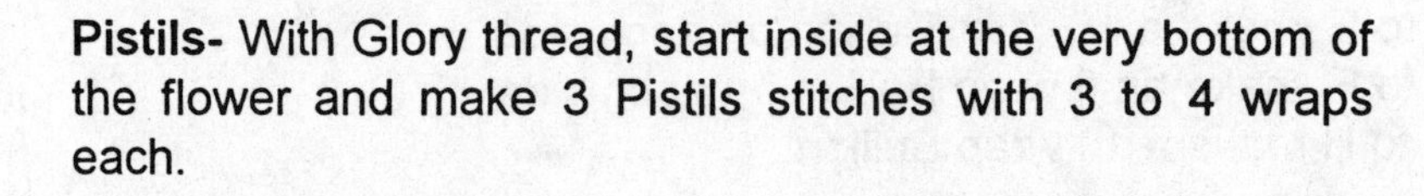
Calyx- With the same thread as the stems, make a 15 wrap Bullion from D to E. Under the first Bullion, make another one with 10 wraps.

Black Eyed Susan

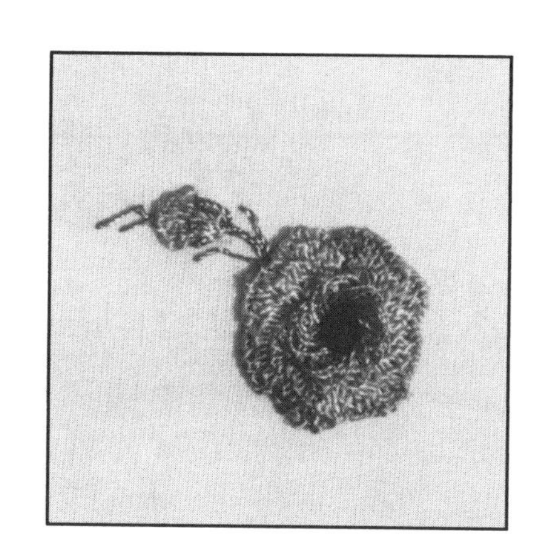

Lola, Bouclé and Glory - French Knots, Chain stitch, Buttonhole, Lazy Daisy, and Hopper stitch.

1- With Lola thread, the same color as Bouclé, come up at the edge of the center and make rows of Chain stitch going around the petals leaving the center open.
2- Using Bouclé thread, come up at the center and make Buttonhole stitches over the Chain stitch to the edge of the flower. Make the stitches very close together.
Center- With Glory thread, make Hopper stitches around the center edge without pulling the stitches tight to form loops. Fill the center with French Knots.

Bud- With Bouclé thread, make Buttonhole stitches. All stitches come out from A and radiate to the top. Using the same thread as the stems, make 2 small branches with Couching stitch coming out from the top of the bud.

Calyx- With the same thread as used for the stems, start at A and make 3 Lazy Daisy stitches into the bud.

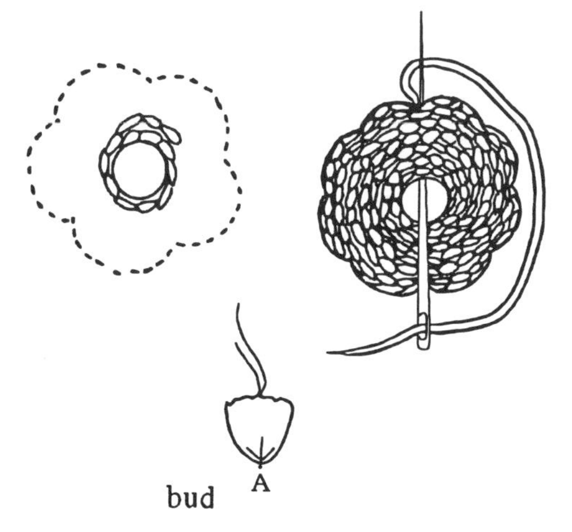

Almond Blossom

Bouclé and Glory - Loop, Pistil, French Knot, and Cast-on stitch.

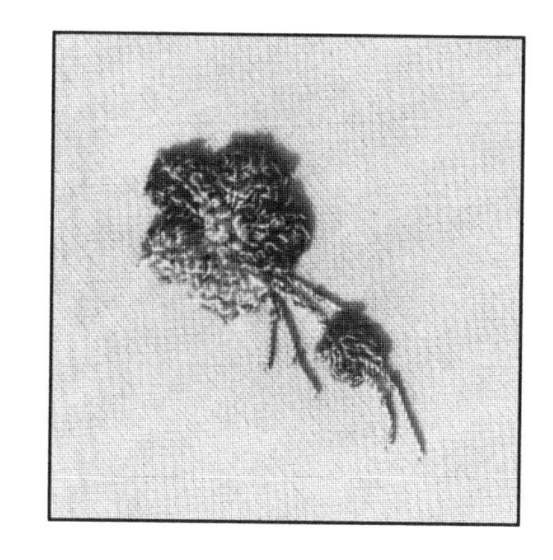

With Bouclé thread, make 2 bars in each petal from the center to the edge. Come up through the fabric on the left side of one of the bars. Slide the needle under the bar without catching the fabric. Following instructions for Loop stitch, go under the bars to fill the circle.

Center- With Glory thread, make 3 pistils for each petal coming from the center. Fill the center with French Knots.

Bud- Make one petal. Using the same thread as the stems, make 2 branches in Couching stitch starting at the center of the circle.

Calyx- A Cast-on from A to B with 8 stitches.

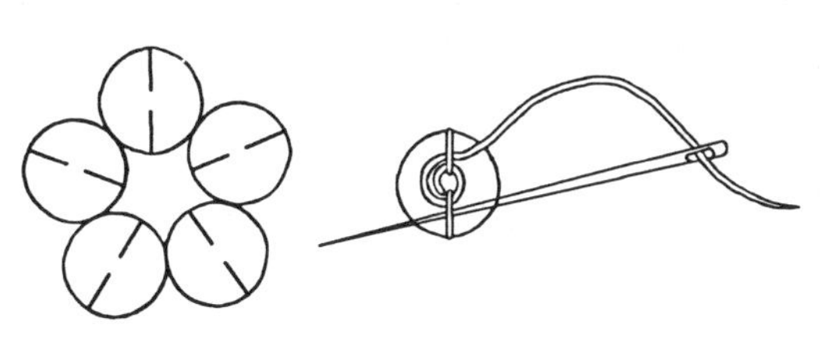

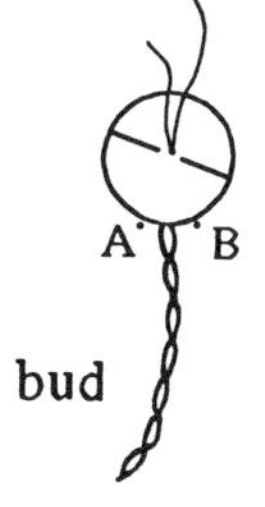

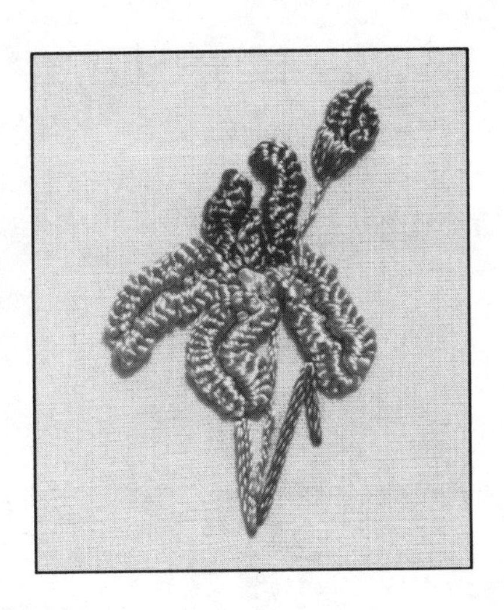

Bearded Iris

Nova and Iris - French Knots, Cast-on and Bullion stitch.

Petals- With Nova thread and a yarn darner needle, begin each petal in the center at A. Make a cast-on stitch from A to B with eight casts, from A to C with 12 casts, and A to D with 15 casts. Secure the petals in place along the line with a small straight stitch (1).
The three bottom petals are each a double petal consisting of two cast-on stitches. A to E, A to F and A to G are made with 22 casts. Come up along the line catching both cast-ons on the edge and bring them close together in two or three places.

Center- With Iris thread, fill the center (A) with French knots and make an additional 8 to 10 along the center of each petal (2).

Bud- A bud is simply two petals side by side with eight casts each stitched from A to B. Make a few small branches coming out from the top.

Calyx- Using the same thread as the branches, make several straight stitches into the bud.

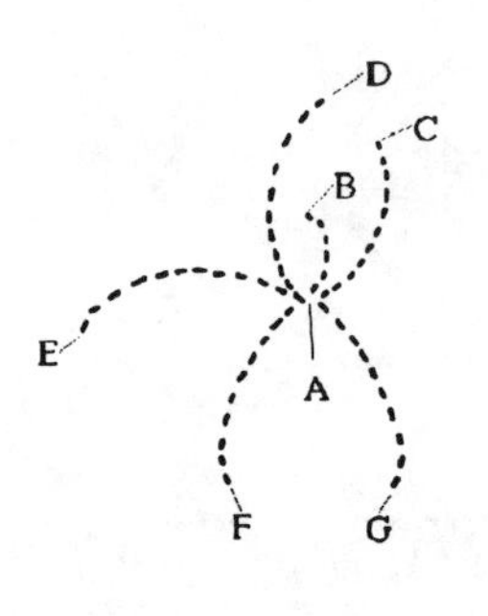

1

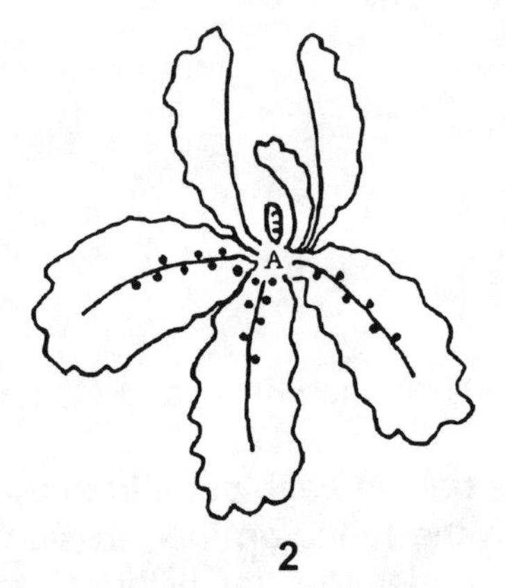

2

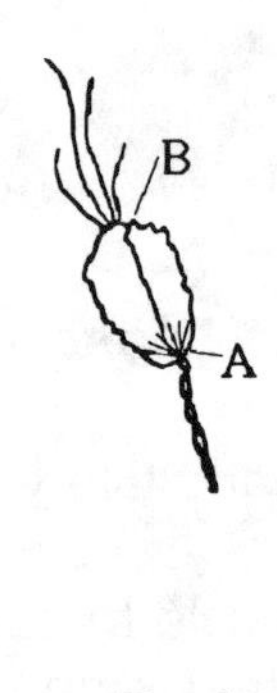

Bud

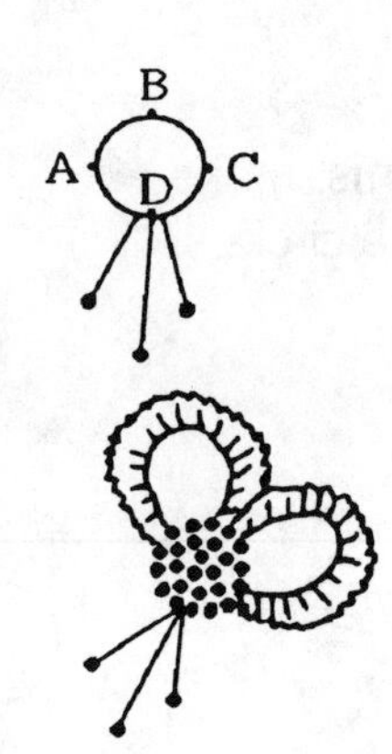

Snowberry

Lola and Glory - Cast-on, Turkey and Pistil stitch.

Petals- With Lola thread, fill the circle with turkey stitches.
With a contrasting color, make a cast-on stitch from A to B with 45 casts and from B to C with 45 casts.

Center- Several Pistil stitches coming out from D.

Mardi Gras Butterfly

Iris, Glory and Frost - Herringbone, Chained Bullion, Stem, Double Cast-on, Bullion, Pistil, Couching, and Straight stitch.

Wings- With Iris thread starting at the top of the head at A, fill the area with herringbone stitch to B. Come up again at A and make herringbone stitches to C. Come up at D and stitch to E and then stitch from F to G.
With Iris thread starting at H, make chained bullion stitches with eight wraps each along the outer edge of the wings. Outline the inner edge with stem stitch (1).

Body- Using Frost thread, make a double cast-on stitch from I to J with thirty casts (15 casts on each side of the needle) (2).

Head- With Frost thread, follow the same instructions and the number of wraps for a Rolled Rose.

Inside the Wings- With Glory thread, make several pistil stitches with six wraps each. All stitches start at the bottom of the wings from K, L and M and radiate to the top (2).

Antennae- With Glory thread, make couching stitches starting at the top of the head following the curves.

Legs- Make straight stitches with Glory thread.

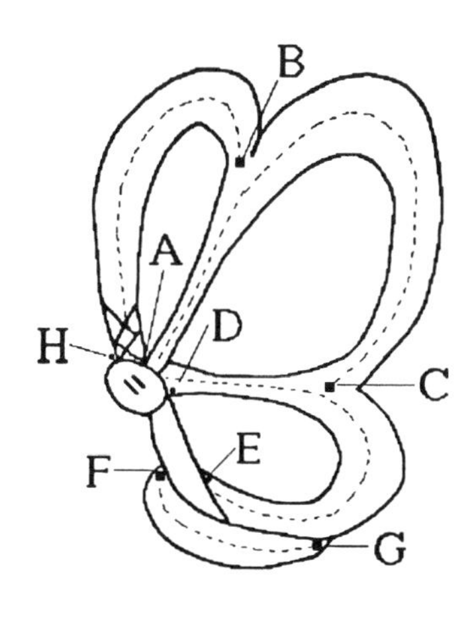

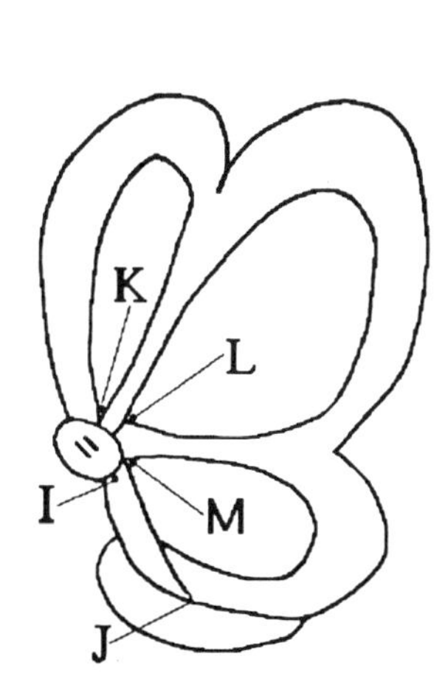

Bottom Ribbon

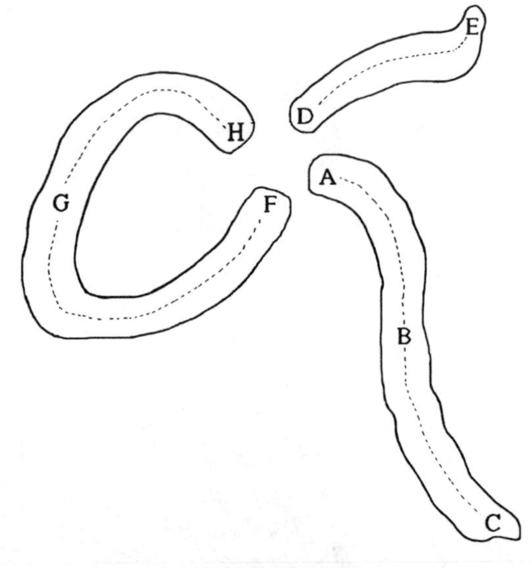

Top Ribbon

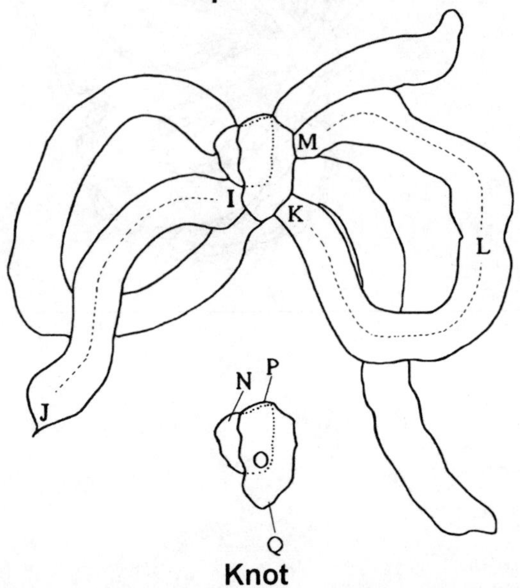

Bow

Iris - Cast-on and Detached Bullion stitch.

You will need a flat strip of plastic 3 or 4 inches long and 1/4" wide and a long needle.

Thread two strands of Iris on the needle and tie a knot at one end. Working the bow in sections, follow the chart below for the amount of casts needed for each section.
For each section, begin as you would for a cast-on stitch. Gather the fabric together between the two points you will be stitching. Lay the plastic strip over the needle and cast over the needle and strip combination making certain that the casts "hug" the strip and the needle together. When you have the number of casts made, hold on to them and pull the strip out from the casts. Hold on to the casts and pull the needle through. Straighten out the fabric and lay the ribbon down in place. Secure the ribbon along the edge by making a few catching stitches through the fabric. If you like a very loose look to the ribbon, make less casts per section or, if a "well packed" look is desired, add more.

Bottom		Top	
A to B:	40 Casts	I to J:	60 Casts
B to C:	40 Casts	K to L:	60 Casts
D to E:	40 Casts	L to M:	50 Casts
F to G:	60 Casts		
G to H:	50 Casts		

Knot- From N to O, make 15 casts and from P to Q, 20 casts. Stitch the edges of the knot the same way as the edges of the bow.

Edges- Do the edges of the top ribbon first and then the edges of the bottom. Do the edges of the knot last.
Catch the edge of the cast-on stitch and a very small bite of the fabric. Make a six wrap detached bullion. Pull the wraps through and continue making bullions about 1/8" apart.
When doing the edges of the bottom ribbon, do not make bullions over the top ribbon.

Pine Cone

Lola - Cast-on stitch.

Start each seed by taking a small bite of fabric at the top from A to B. Make the five top seeds with 22 casts each and the three bottom ones with 15 casts each.

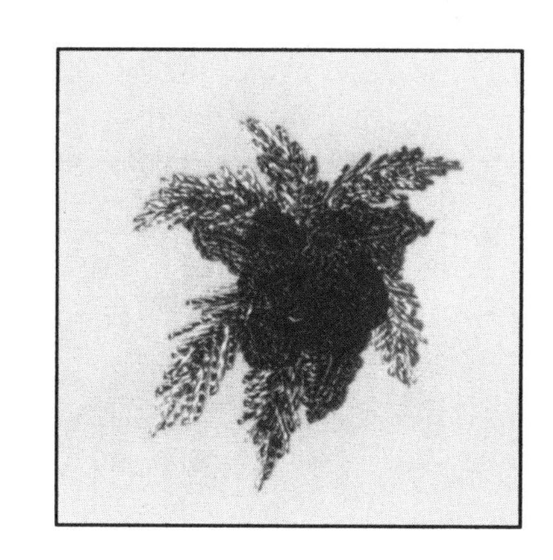

Acorns

Iris - French Knots, Stem stitch, Bullion, Detached Bullion and Padded Satin stitch.

Fill the area with diagonal satin stitches that are very close together (1). Cross-hatch a second diagonal layer above the first (2). For the top layer, radiate a series of straight stitches from the base outward (3).

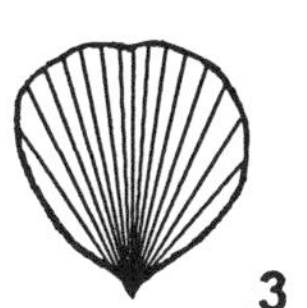

Acorn Variations

A. Fill the top part with French knots over the satin stitch.

B. Make bullions with six wraps each in a row over the satin stitch.

C. Make a stem stitch from A to B very close to the satin stitch. Starting at B and using the stem stitch for an anchor, make seven detached bullion stitches with six wraps each. Make two rows the same way. The third row should be done with eight detached bullions.

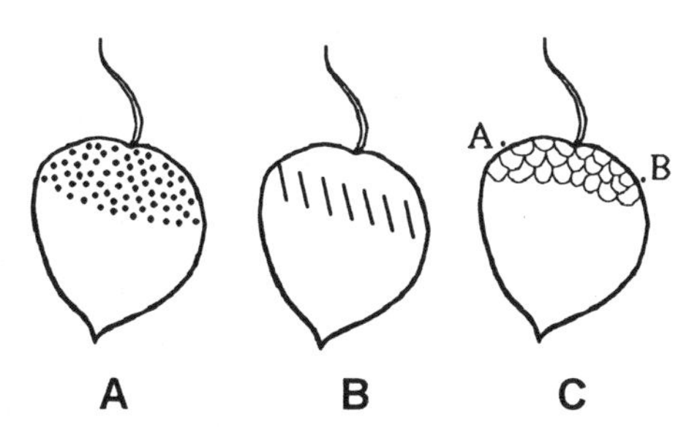

Nobel Poinsettia

Lola and Iris - Knotted Double Cast-on and French Knots.

Petals- Come up at the edge of the center at the base of any petal. Insert the needle down at the tip, then up at the base. Follow the instructions for the Knotted Cast-on stitch wrapping four times around the needle. On the fifth wrap, go with the needle through the loop.
Make eight Knotted Cast-on stitches; four on each side. Then, make four stitches; two on each side wrapping only twice around the needle. The third time, go inside the loop.
Make four single Cast-ons; two on each side. Pull the stitches tight against the fabric to bunch them up together, then pull the needle and thread through. Go down at the tip and secure.
Center- With Iris thread, fill the center with French Knots.

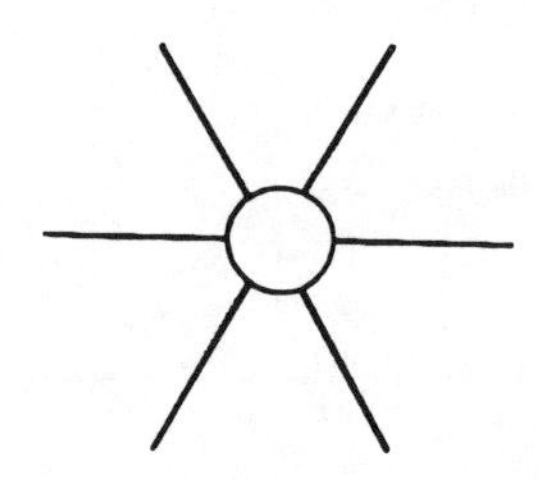

Latin Poinsettia

Iris - French Knots and Alternating Sating stitch.

Petals- Come up at the end of the petal vein. Follow the instructions for Alternating Satin stitch graduating down on the petal. Make the stitches slanted and very close together. Work all the petals the same way.

Center- With Iris thread, fill the center with French Knots.

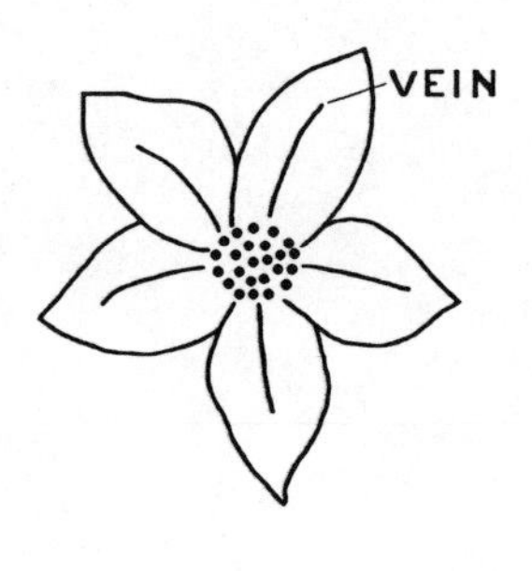

Color and thread guide for Hanging Bouquet

Print #1607

1. Stems & branches, Lola #216.
2. Bow, Iris #221.
3. Field Flowers (Wisteria style), Iris #028.
4. Regular Leaves, Iris #216.
5. Almond Blossom, Bouclé #146. Center, Glory #166.
6. Buttonhole Leaf (two layers), Iris #110
7. African Daisy, outer edge of petal, Lola #065. Center of petal, Lola #211. Flower center, Lola #085
8. African Daisy, small bud, Lola #065. Calyx, Lola #216
9. African Daisy, large bud, Lola #065 & Iris #211. Calyx, Iris #110
10. Eucalyptus Flower and Bud, Lola #034. Pistil, Glory #166
11. Picotee Dahlia, Lola #104. Center, Iris #124 & #206
12. Picotee Dahlia, large and small Bud, Lola #104
13. Feather Leaf, Iris #227
14. Maria's Rose and Buds, Lola #070
15. Petite Fuchsia and Buds, Nova #030. Petals, Nova #169. Pistils, Glory #169.

Fine growth, Glory #051.

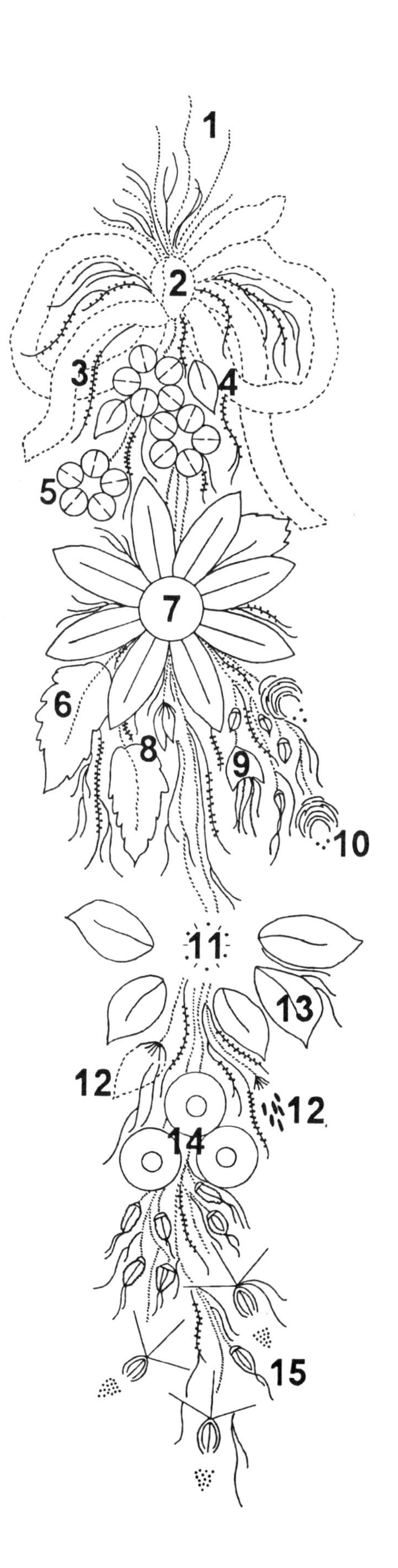

Color and thread guide for Nine Flower Sampler

Print #1816

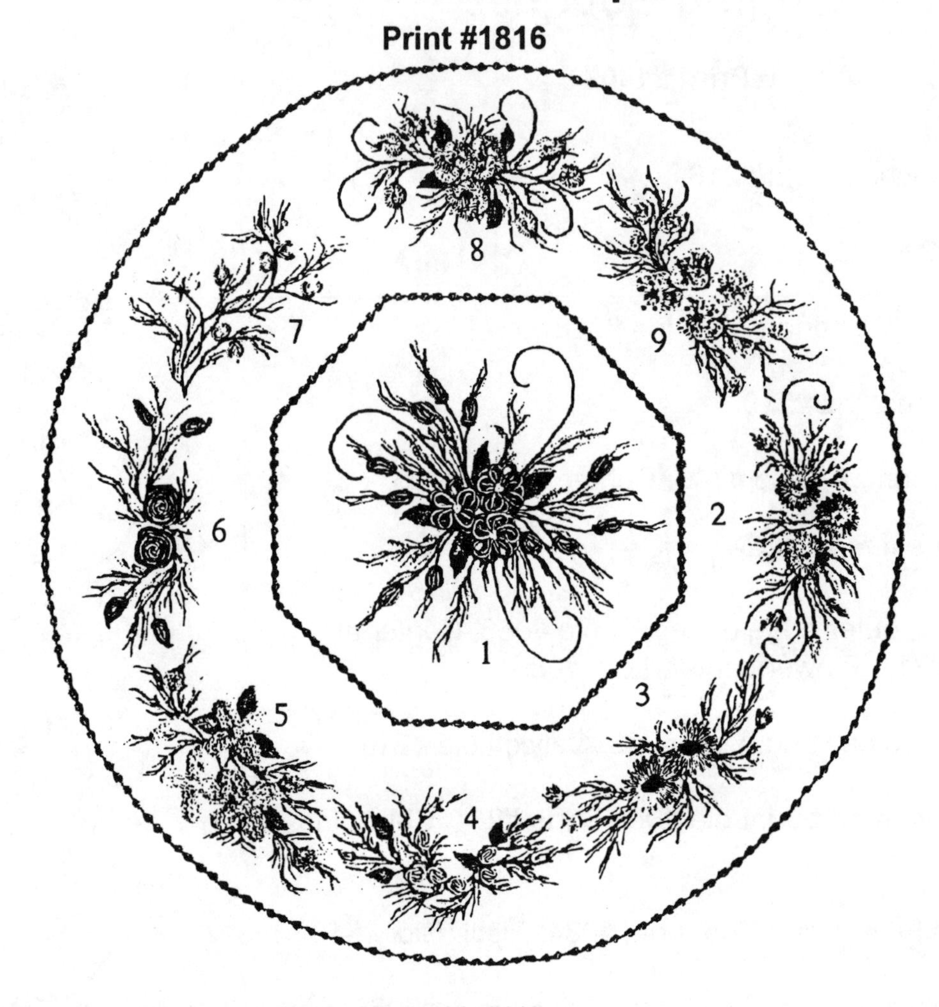

1. Japanese Violet. Petals and Buds, Lola #009. Center, Iris #119.
   Stems, Iris #216. Regular Leaves and Branches, Iris #045. Field Flowers, Glory #000. Fine Growth, Glory #024.
2. Geron Daisy. Petals and Buds, Iris #030. Center, Glory #000, #030.
   Stems and Branches, Lola #216. Field Flowers, Glory #000. Fine Growth, Glory #048.
3. Knotted Lazy Daisy. Petals and Buds, Lola #039. Center, Iris #210.
   Stems and Branches, Iris #110. Field Flowers, Glory #000. Fine Growth, Glory #024.
4. Rolled Rose. Flower and Buds, Lola #004.
   Regular Leaves, Stems and Branches, Frost #165. Field Flowers, Glory #000. Fine Growth, Glory #048.
5. Bouclé Rose. Flower and Buds, Bouclé #072. Center, Glory #000.
   Regular Leaves,Stems and Branches, Iris #110. Field Flowers, Glory #000. Fine Growth, Glory #024.
6. Bullion Rose. Flower and Buds, Lola #065.
   Stems and Branches, Lola #216. Field Flowers, Glory #000. Fine Growth, Glory #048.
7. Creeping Flower. Lola #037. Pistils, Glory #081.
   Stems and Branches, Iris #110. Field Flowers, Glory #000. Fine Growth, Glory #024.
8. Cast-on Flower. Flower and Buds, Lola #104. Center, Iris #210.
   Regular Leaves, Stems and Branches, Frost #216. Fine Growth, Glory #048.
9. Peach Blossom. Flower and Buds, Nova #004. Center, Glory #010.
   Stems and Branches, Iris #110. Field Flowers, Glory #000. Fine Growth, Glory #024.

Borders. Palestrina stitch, Nova #120.

MAIN COLOR LIST

Variegated Colors

002	Grey & White
003	Light Yellow & White
005	Salmon & White
008	Medium Yellow & Marigold
010	Tan & Light Yellow
011	Dark Pink & Blue
012	Blue & Lavender
013	Light Pink & Light Yellow
014	Light Blue & Light Yellow
016	Light Salmon & Grey
017	Light Pink & Lt. Violet *Pastels*
019	Yellow & Purple
020	Dark Jade & Medium Burgundy
021	Pink, Blue & Green *Pastels*
022	Yellow & Orange
023	Coral & Blue
026	Pink, Blue & Yellow *Pastels*
027	Dark Pink & Burgundy
028	Grey, Beige, Peach, & Lavender *Pastels*
031	Light Pink, Lavender & White
033	Blue, Yellow & Orange
035	Orange, Yellow & White
036	Blue & White
037	Lavender, Salmon & Blue
039	Orange, Lt. Yellow & Lt. Brown
044	Yellow, Brown & Green
045	Green & Brown
047	Sage Green & Grey
052	Fuchsia & Violet
054	Pink, Yellow & Lavender *Pastels*
055	Light Blue, Salmon & Light Brown
056	Red & White
057	Royal Blue & Dark Orchid
058	Blue & Green
060	Light Blue/Grey & Natural
061	Green & Red Ochre
064	Yellow & Brown
085	Light Apricot & Tan
090	Light Pink & White
091	Light Lavender & White
092	Light Blue & White
093	Pink & Light Blue

Shaded Colors

001	Medium to Light Blue
004	Pale to Light Pink
006	Pale to Light Antique Rose
007	Pale to Light Grape
009	Dark to Medium Tangerine
015	Medium to Light Salmon
018	Light to Pale Rose
024	Light to Pale Sea Green
025	Medium to Light Gray
030	Medium to Light Cinnamon
034	Light to Pale Periwinkle
040	Medium to Light Hunter Green
041	Medium to Light Plum Blossom
042	Whisper to Pale Sea Green
043	Light to Pale Fuchsia
048	Pale to Light Kelly Green
049	Light to Pale Avocado
050	Medium to Dark Avocado
051	Pale to Light Moss Green
053	Light to Medium Avocado
059	Dark to Medium Chocolate
062	Medium to Light Sage Green
063	Pale to Whisper Turquoise
065	Dark to Light Cranberry
069	Medium to Dark Straw
070	Whisper to Pale Orchid
071	Dark to Light Turquoise
072	Dark to Light Apricot
073	Dark to Light Golden Yellow
074	Dark to Light Fuchsia
075	Whisper to Med. Christmas Red
076	Dark to Light Royal Blue
077	Medium to Light Grape
078	Medium to Light Tangerine
079	Dark to Light Jade
080	Dark to Pale Avocado
081	Medium to Dark Eggshell
082	Pale to Light Blue/Grey
083	Medium to Pale Hot Pink
086	Medium to Light Mulberry
087	Medium to Dark Cocoa
088	Pale to Light Gray
089	Pale to Medium Russet
094	Dark to Light Plum
095	Pale to Whisper Moss Green
096	Whisper to Pale Apricot
097	Light to Pale Pearl
098	Whisper to Pale Violet
100	Light to Medium Baby Blue
101	Light to Medium Christmas Red
102	Dark to Medium Ecru
103	Light to Medium Royal Blue
104	Medium to Dark Peach
105	Dark to Medium Violet
106	Dark to Medium Golden Yellow
107	Medium to Light Orchid
108	Pale to Light Yellow
109	Medium to Light Kelly Green
110	Dark to Light Olive Green

Solid Colors

000	White
111	Baby Blue
112	Light Sky Blue
113	Yellow
114	Light Yellow
115	Cantaloupe
116	Light Antique Rose
117	Violet
118	Apricot
119	Peach
120	Chocolate
121	Moss Green
122	Light Rust
123	Blue
124	Light Grey
125	Lavender
126	Light Brown
127	Orchid
128	Rust
129	Gold
130	Egg Shell
131	Hot Pink
132	Grey
133	Tangerine
134	Light Yellow
135	Pale Pink
136	Light Violet
137	Dark Orchid
138	Straw
139	Dark Sky Blue
140	Light Turquoise
141	Dark Mulberry
142	Mulberry
143	Light Mulberry
144	Navy
145	Slate Blue
146	Light Blue/Grey
147	Blue/Grey
148	Jade
149	Dark Avocado
150	Dark Moss Green
151	Pale Avocado
152	Christmas Red
153	Pink
154	Red
155	Dark Pink
156	Teal
157	Burgundy
160	Dark Emerald Green
161	Slate Green
162	Light Lime
163	Antique Rose
164	Mint Green
165	Light Sage Green
166	Light Ecru
167	Sage Green
168	Pale Apricot
169	Pale Strawberry
170	Dark Sea Green
171	Light Orchid
200	Dark Tangerine
201	Royal Blue
202	Golden Tan
203	Golden Yellow
204	Fuchsia
205	Ruby
206	Black
207	Dark Grape
208	Poppy
209	Scarlet
210	Brown
211	Dark Tuscany
212	Turquoise
213	Bright Yellow/Green
214	Hunter Green
215	Avocado
216	Light Moss Green
217	Bright Green
218	Light Fuchsia
219	Light Periwinkle
220	Periwinkle
221	Light Tuscany
222	Light Beige
223	Beige
224	Pale Turquoise
225	Light Sable
226	Sable
227	Pale Sea Green

Ciré is not available in all colors.
Consult your dealer about current availability.

Index